MW00415631

PINSTRIPE SUITS TO PRISON BLUES

How an Entrepreneur went from Millionaire to Bankruptcy and Prison Only to Return a Stronger Person Dedicating His Life to Helping Others with the Power of Faith Family and Friends

Michael R Holley

Contact Michael
To Book Michael for your event or consulting, call
(844) 446-7338
For more information, go to
www.michaelholley.com

© by Michael R. Holley

Published by Hopeful Publishing Company, Inc. Lakeland, FL For volume discounts,
institutional sales, corporate events or promotional use send an email to info@
hopefulpublishing.com or use form on www.hopefulpublishing.com

Scripture taken from the Holy Bible, NEW INTERNATIONAL VERSION®. Copyright
© 1973, 1978, 1984 by Biblica, Inc. All rights reserved worldwide. Used by permission.

Hopeful Publishing Company, Inc.
P.O. Box 7517
Lakeland, FL 33807

Note to Readers:
In some instances people or companies portrayed in this book are illustrative
examples based on author experiences, they are not intended to represent a
particular person or organization.
All efforts were made to produce a perfect book, however we acknowledge that errors
or omissions are possible and, ask for your forgiveness.

Library of Congress Cataloging-in-Publication Data

Holley, Michael R. 1960-

Pinstripe Suits to Prison Blues, memoir, self-help, spiritual, a living guide to overcoming
obstacles and adversity. Helping others see their life from a different perspective and
helping others along the way.

ISBN: 0986228605
ISBN 13: 9780986228605
ISBN 13: 9780986228612 eBook
Library of Congress Control Number: 2014921385
Hopeful Publishing Company, Inc, Lakeland FL

TO MY WIFE HOPE, I LOVE YOU AND THANK YOU FOR ALL
THE SUPPORT, CHEERING, LOVE AND PASSION FOR THIS
PROJECT AND OUR LIVES!

CONTENTS

Foreword xiii

Introduction xvii

Chapter 1   The Early Years 1

Chapter 2   From Ship to Showroom Floor 13

Chapter 3   Small Town Boy Becomes Big Town Manager 25

Chapter 4   A General Manager in a Strange Place 33

Chapter 5   The Opportunity of a Lifetime 39

Chapter 6   The Growth to Executive Manager 45

Chapter 7   The Loss of a Mentor and Purchase
             of a Business 55

Chapter 8   Building an Empire and Family 65

Chapter 9   The Beginning of the End 75

Chapter 10   The Ending of an Empire 93

Chapter 11   Criminal Prosecution 99

Chapter 12   Prison Blues 105

Chapter 13   The Prison System Not Seen on TV 115

Chapter 14   Days, Weeks, and Months Pass Through
             the System 137

Chapter 15   New Souls to Learn From 143

Chapter 16   A Second Chance at Enlightenment 155

Chapter 17   A Semi-Free but Enlightened New Man 165

Chapter 18   Back to Business and Seeking to Help Others 171

Acknowledgements 181

FOREWORD

Pinstripe Suits to Prison Blues is the true and unvarnished story of the remarkable rise, fall and ultimate reinvention of my longtime friend and fellow "Car Dealer" Michael Holley.

Michael and I came to the car business from very different circumstances. I was born into a successful automobile family and handed my opportunity, while Michael created his opportunity by sweat, a ferocious work ethic, dogged determination, an amazing innate instinct, and the help of a few "Guardian Angels" along the way.

His, in many ways, is the quintessential American success story. Rising from modest roots, Michael stumbled from his successful career as a boat captain to the car business almost by chance, and against all odds began his meteoric rise to the top. Powered by talent, drive, his ability to get people to believe in him, and fearless risk taking, he made the improbable journey from car salesmen to the owner of multiple automobile dealerships, community leader, philanthropist and political power broker. It was the fearless risk taking at the wrong time that would begin a chain of events that caused it all to crash down and propel Michael on a very different journey.

The bone crushing recession that began in 2008 hit car dealerships with a ferocity that is hard to understand if you didn't live through it. Many great operators went out of business as panic took hold among consumers, and credit for the average car buyer completely dried up. All car dealers were in completely uncharted waters as we struggled to survive against economic forces largely beyond our control. It was a terrifying time, as many dealerships, mine included, teetered on the edge of solvency. It is hard to describe the feeling of watching everything you worked for your entire adult life crash and burn before your eyes. It was in this frightening and chaotic environment that Michael, trying to save his dealerships, made a couple of decisions that would ultimately cost him his fortune and his freedom.

This is the story of the Journey that took Michael from humble roots to the pinnacle of success, to the depths of despair, and ultimately to a new and deeper understanding of who he was and what he wanted to be. It is the story of a good man, who made mistakes and paid a huge price. That he survived intact, discovered the positive lessons in an unimaginably bad situation, and found a way to channel it all into a force for good is a true testament to the toughness, grit and determination of my friend. The story is compelling, as are the life lessons that jump from every page. This is his story...
Jim Quinlan

INTRODUCTION

This is the story about an uneducated yet hard working man born in north Florida of humble beginnings. This book covers some forty years of the life and times of an aspiring entrepreneur even before he knew what the term meant. The following is the unbelievable story of the career and work ethic of a future deal maker, political activist, radio talk show host, and philanthropist who would lose everything material.

With an inside look at the companies, businesses small enough to let fail, as well as the many lives that it touched, you will see and hear the stories of this self-made business person who made deals that could only be dreamed of with an impossible net worth that went up in smoke in a matter of days. Then after losing almost everything, he would in turn lose his freedom and be sent to prison. While prison is awful, you get an inside look at a world you have heard or read about, seen on television, maybe read in fiction books.

You will be taken on a journey inside the lives of people and places that the author would have never met had it not been for these circumstances; a look into how someone could become so rich in the love of people that money no longer mattered; a look into the building of relationships; a look into yourself and the situations you or your loved ones have been in. And you'll wonder if given a chance to reset, start over, reboot, what would you do with it? Would you take that chance to teach or reteach yourself all that you thought you had learned in a lifetime to reach out to people and help? Would you educate yourself with the reading of over one hundred nonfiction self-help and biography books to learn from the best, brightest, and most tried men, women and circumstances in our history. Would you take this opportunity to see the limitless ability to expand the mind and personal knowledge with unlimited time to read, study, and listen to others in a situation where many go mad, or worse, commit suicide. Would you have the ability to see what before could not be seen, to hear what before were just words, and to know what you could not possibly have been known: that to expand one's knowledge is only limited to the time and energy that you are willing to invest in such knowledge; that you were born with a free will and an inner wisdom that belongs to you to be accessed and exercised well after learning or feeling that you have it; to see the power of building lasting relationships that will last forever unless destroyed by your own misjudgment; to come to covet the love of faith, family, and friends that becomes your only true treasure and worldly possession.

This is a powerful story, told with southern charm, that will make for great fireside chats and give you an introspective about situations you may have heard about but never experienced. Please enjoy and spread your knowledge as you see the life and times of those that have risen and fallen, been imprisoned and resurrected to be more than anyone thought a convicted felon could be.

As you read this book you might ask, as so many have, why write the book? Simple, I have a story to tell, an untold story encompassing all the above and much more. The real reason for writing the book is to touch the heart and soul of an up and coming entrepreneur or a seasoned veteran looking to make a course adjustment. I have seen and been exposed to a world that most have not seen. I felt compelled to tell the story, share the lessons, and hopefully spark a desire in someone, anyone that might want to be all that they thought they could not. I want to offer a second chance to someone that thought there were none to be had. To touch or save a lost soul that may yet have the best to offer the world but are standing in their own way, creating their own bad luck while opportunities are flying over their head. This book was the hardest business thing I have ever done. I hope it helps you touch others, to be all that you can be and take a few others with you down the road of your destined success. You are a success story waiting to be written. Now let's write it!

"By failing to prepare, you are preparing to fail."

— Benjamin Franklin

1

THE EARLY YEARS

I was born in Panama City Florida on December 26, 1960 at 1:07 a.m. My mother was in labor all Christmas day and still loves me, go figure. I grew up in the small town of Lynn Haven, in the panhandle of Florida, about sixty miles south of the Alabama line and about ten miles north of the Gulf of Mexico. The Gulf of Mexico and the sandy white beaches of Panama City Beach, referred to as "The World's Most Beautiful Beaches," were my playground. This very unique stretch of beaches goes from St. George Island to Pensacola Florida, and through some miracle of nature the beaches are as white as processed sugar, known well by spring breakers and families from Alabama, Georgia, Tennessee, and around the world.

Life was simple: fishing, hunting, football, baseball, Fourth of July, church, big Christmas gatherings, and family/friend get-to-gethers. My mom, dad, sister, and I were a close family, as were our extended families. Every Sunday after church, we went to one of my grandmothers, aunts, or cousins houses for lunch and family gatherings. As much as I enjoyed Fourth of July, football, family gatherings, dove hunting, and fishing, what I really desired to do was go to work.

From the time I was a very little boy, I accompanied my grand-father, Capt. A. R. Holley, on his boat, The Red Fin VI (a sixty-five-foot party/head fishing boat). He was a huge man, and many were scared of him, including me. But to my sister and me, he was a gentle, caring fisherman that could catch and cook fish as good as any on earth. We also went with our friends, the Davises, on their boats, fishing and scalloping in the summer and oystering in the winter. My uncle, Richard Holley, would work for Davis Queen Fleet and captain a number of their boats when he returned from the Air Force where he served during Vietnam. Every summer, I fished with my grandfather on his boat until the time of his death on board that very boat in 1969. Until I could work on the boats, I mowed lawns, worked at gas stations, rode with my other grandfather on a uniform route counting dirty uniforms and helping line up his load, as well as working with my own dad pumping fuel oil and cleaning gas stations. I did other odd jobs, but what I really wanted to do was to be at sea. When I finally did get to go to work, it was not working at all, but a dream come true. I worked, played, met people, and most of all learned about boats, fishing, people, and the Gulf of Mexico; and I was paid to do it.

I worked on board the New Dixie Queen (a sixty-five-foot party/head boat) for six dollars per half-day trip. Trips ran from 7 a.m. to noon, and from 1 p.m. to 6 p.m. I could make twelve dollars a day, plus the occasional tip, if I worked both trips. From the first time that I worked on board the New Dixie Queen I was hooked.

I remember that first day as if it was yesterday. It was a beautiful calm day in the Gulf, and the captain was my uncle, Capt. Richard Holley. As others talked about how many days they had worked without a day off, or how many hours they had put in, I could not have been more thrilled to be there. This was the beginning of what I thought was my lifelong career, and the fulfillment of a lifelong, as short of a life as I had lived so far, dream.

As the years went on, I continued to work on the boats in the summer and play football in the fall: first for the Lynn Haven

Raiders peewee team (eight- to ten-year-olds), then the Lynn Haven Raiders midget team, then Mowat Junior High Mustangs, and lastly the Mosley Dolphins, my high school team. I played for the first peewee team that Lynn Haven had. Our first year they used lipstick to make out numbers on oversized T shirts; then the second year they sprayed them on with stencils and orange spray paint. We were terrible in those first few years, but what a group of guys. Many of us would play together through high school and remain lifelong friends. My coach, Bill Hughes, became a mentor of mine until I lost track of him. My father, Randy Holley, would follow Coach Hughes to coach the Raiders. In ten years of coaching, he and his assistant coach and close friend, Bobbie Dancy, would become one of the winningest peewee teams in the United States.

It was an incredibly rewarding childhood as my parents, Joyce and Randy Holley, basically let me work as much as I wanted to. In the winter and spring I worked at gas stations, at a farm and garden supply store, and mowed lawns until it was too cold. One spring, I worked at a sky-ride tourist attraction on Panama City Beach. Sometimes I worked until two in the morning, even on school nights. That job only lasted a few weeks. I was thirteen years old and in eighth grade; I am not sure who was more ready for me to be done with it, me or my dad. I do remember my junior high school English teacher coming out to visit one night. She was terrified of heights, but took the ride anyway. We were a little busy, and I was on the back platform in the woods where I turned around the sky ride gauntlet and there was no room to park one. So as soon as the next one arrived, I had to send her on her scared way. Wow, how many teachers would do that for their worst student? That meant so much to me; and since I am writing about it forty years later, you see the impression it made.

While I worked on the boats those summers, I had daily interactions with people. As the summer progressed, I met hundreds and hundreds of people from all walks of life. I was beginning to learn and to understand (read) people at a very young age: when they were happy, when they were concerned, when I was doing something they didn't understand, or maybe even when they wanted to ask me a question but didn't. As I became closer with some of these people, it became very common for them to tell me that I had a special gift of communicating with people, a very positive attitude, a special outlook on life, and I was going to be a great success. For a long time, I was not sure what they meant, what they saw in me, or even what some of the compliments meant. One time, this nice lady told me she bet I was a real Don Juan. I had no idea what she was talking about, or even if it was a compliment.

Besides my uncle, I had a number of mentors on the boats and around the docks. One was Wally Helmke, he was sort of my own personal Old Man and the Sea. As legend has it, they say he was a retired electrician from Tennessee, but it seemed to me he had been around the sea at least a hundred years. He would answer any question I had, as if he had nothing else to do in the world. He taught me how to tie knots, work on rod and reels, cut and prepare bait, ice down fish, sharpen knives, clean the boat, and as the junior guy in the crew that also meant cleaning the heads (bathrooms). The half-day boat trips had a lot of first time boaters, which meant a lot of sea-sick people, even when it was not that rough. The half-day boat trip meant two trips a day for the crew. That also meant setting up rods and reels, cutting bait, cleaning fish boxes, and yes, cleaning-up the boat twice a day. It was a minor price to pay for being employed and doing what I had dreamed of as early as I could remember—since my first time at sea when I was six months old, so I am told. Many years later, I would take my son out when he was just two weeks old on our boat, the Princess Hope, for a cruise in the Gulf of Mexico and Tampa Bay. He learned to swim before he could walk and loves the sea as much as any Holley ever born.

So one day I asked Wally why people were always telling me that I was special, that I was going to be somebody one day, and that I had a gift? He said, "Well son, it's like this: you're a nice-looking and friendly boy with a big smile who loves his work and the customers that come out here. You're not that bright, so you don't intimidate them, you're very eager, and easy to talk to." I then remembered what my fifth grade teacher, Ms. Harris, told me, "Michael I'm sure you're going to rule the world one day, but right now my job is to get you out of fifth grade, and you've got to learn your multiplication tables." Bright I was not, but loving people and the sea I did.

I spent some time meditating on what Wally had said. At the time I had absolutely no idea what it was, but looking back, I was meditating. I had a tree overlooking the bay about two blocks from my house that I would climb up and spend lots of time watching eagles catch fish, and just being with myself. That was very uncommon for me because I did not like to be alone. I love to be around people and the more people the better, it is as if I draw strength from the interactions. During this time, I came to realize a number of things; one was that I did have a gift, the gift of interacting with and understanding people. I knew very young I was never going to be a PhD or college professor, and I wasn't even sure at that point if I was going to graduate from high school. I spent hours and hours studying the things I did love: people, the sea and running fishing boats. I bought my first boat at thirteen, an old fifteen-foot Cobia with a 55 Evinrude motor. I would launch it into the bay not far from my house with my neighbors riding lawn mower then leave it in the water until my dad got home with the station wagon to get it out.

Almost every summer until I was seventeen years old, I worked as a deckhand on the fishing boats in Panama City. I made extra money on the side, stringing-up what was then called trash fish (fish that would've normally been thrown back or overboard, and considered non-keepers at the time) into strings of about five-foot long. I would then sell them on the dock for five dollars a string to people who could not afford the more sought after, and higher priced, red snapper and black grouper. Some days I would double my pay for the day by doing this. Years later, I learned that one of the ladies I sold fish to would take them to her neighborhood and resell them individually, one fish at a time. That struck me as wrong, but then I guess I was the wholesaler and she was the retailer. Another way I would make extra money was to help tourists that I met around the marina with their own boats. I would also take people fishing, or just tour them around the bay and the Gulf of Mexico. I would use their boat, their gas, eat their food, and they paid me. Sometimes I was paid as much as I normally made in a week, just for being a tour guide and then cleaning their boat. Yes, life was perfect. At some point my boss, Joe Ed Davis, said, "Son, as much fun as you're having, and as many girls as you're meeting, you should be paying me!" That was not far from the truth.

During the winter, after school, I worked at a farm and garden supply store. I also worked at a friend of my dad's gas station. Sometimes I'd close the station at 10 p.m., put the money bag in my belt, and ride my bike home. Those were certainly simpler times. No one even considered that this might be unsafe. At the time, I guess I didn't appreciate how well I was doing financially for a young teenager. I seemed to always have money in my pocket and do not recall ever having to ask my parents for money. I made more than any of the other teens I knew, and in my later teens there were many weeks that my dad said I was making almost as much as him. This helped with my appreciation for money at a young age, though money was never really a goal for me but a tool to do so much more. I understand now how I so under-appreciated the freedom my parents gave me to do all that I was doing. I do not recall how I got around to all these places since I could not drive until I was sixteen years old. At sixteen I bought my mom's Chevy for three hundred fifty dollars cash and was off.

My high school years were great, all except for the part about going to class. I went to school to play football and socialize; and I regret not staying in school and playing football my senior year. The team was not very good, but I had played with some of these guys since peewee. I knew that what I wanted to be in life was a ship's captain, so I saw no need to learn anything else, and for that I was very wrong. I tried to drop out when I was sixteen or seventeen, but I had a guidance counselor who talked me into staying in school and enrolling in a DCT, or Diversified Career Education class so that I could work my last year of school and graduate. Since I could not work on the boats in the wintertime or at a DCT job, I worked at a farm and garden supply store that was owned by the mayor of Panama City. I didn't particularly care for the job, but it did give me a chance to interact with a completely different group of people than on the boats, and I learned about farming supplies and animal feed.

It was after a while working there that I wrecked my car. At the body shop where my car was repaired, I met the girl who would become my first wife. She was so quiet and shy, but man could she paint a car. People were always so amazed by a girl working in a body shop, but they got over it when they say how talented she was. She went on to own her own body shop and become a city commissioner and the mayor of the small town she grew up in.

While getting my car fixed for the second time, the body shop manager asked if I would be interested in learning the assistant manager's position. So towards the end of my senior year in high school, I left the farm and garden supply store and the boats, and became the assistant body shop manager at the local Cadillac GMC dealer. If I had only known this would not be my last interaction with a local car dealership.

I worked there for about a year, learning how to interact with other employees, customers, and insurance companies, and how to deal with a lot of paperwork (something I had never had to worry about before). I did not really know what I was doing and was not respected by the other employees. I also was getting an insight into the corporate world by interacting with General Motors representatives on warranty problems, and with customers who always wanted things done correctly and quickly. These would come back to be valuable teaching lessons later on in my career.

After doing this for about a year, my uncle, Capt. Richard Holley, whom I had worked under for so many years on the party/head boats, asked me if I would like to return to the fishing boats, apprentice under him, and get my Captain's License? He had obtained his own charter fishing boat, the "A. R. Holley", which was named after his and my dad's father (and, of course, my grandfather) who had died at sea when I was eight years old. The next year and a half, I worked with my uncle on his charter boat while studying for my captain's license. (The license that I wanted to obtain was a 100 ton Masters license.) For this license you have to be nineteen years old and have seven hundred and thirty, eight-hour days at sea. That takes many years to obtain, and most do not have that much time at sea until later in life. I had accumulated enough time to take the exam right after my nineteenth birthday. I took the exam three times, and failed all three times. Then I enrolled in Sea School, which was based in St. Petersburg, Florida. I took their class in Pensacola, Florida. While taking the class, I stayed with my cousins, Alma and Johnny Jackson. He is a retired Navy man and his wife is my mom's cousin. (My mom and her husband, Mel Snowden, paid for the school.) I passed the test after completing the course, and at the age of nineteen, had my hundred-ton Masters license. I was now Captain Michael R. Holley, or as I was called around the docks, A.R.'s or Capt. Holley's boy. Most of the time, I never knew if they were talking about my dad, my uncle, or my grandfather. I would just say "Yes sir."

One day I was moving the A.R. Holley, a fifty-five-foot boat, by myself to get fuel, bait, and ice for the next day's trip. The wind was blowing hard, and I thought this is not going to be fun. I maneuvered the boat through a narrow canal, eased up to the dock, quickly ran to the back deck to tie up to the small dock before the boat blew back into the channel. All the while Mr. Joel, who ran a local fish market and had been a friend of my grandfather's, watched me, offering no help I might add. When I finished and was out of breath, he said, "You're A.R.'s grandboy. Ain't ya?" I replied, "Yes Sir." He said, "I can tell." I think there was a compliment in there somewhere. I loaded the boat, returned it to the slip, and tied it up again, all by myself. I spent a few more months working for my uncle and then applied to Marine Transportation Services, a company of oil supply and crew boats.

I would spend roughly the next two and a half years working with my uncle on his charter boat, and in the oil fields of the Gulf of Mexico on the Motor Vessel Janie D., a 127 foot crew boat. We worked in the oil fields for two weeks on and two weeks off, so during my off time I helped my uncle. During this time my dad, Iver Randall Holley, or Randy as everyone called him, who had not worked on boats during his adult life, would get his Captain's license and go on to become the most senior captain with the same company before his retirement in 2006. The family that owned Marine Transportation Services, based in Panama City, FL, was the Davis family that had owned Davis Queen Fleet, the fleet of head/party boats that I worked on during my early teenage years. The crew boat, or marine transportation business, was run by Grover Davis, another great mentor. His brother, Joe Ed, my boss at Davis Queen Fleet, is deceased as of this writing, but Grover is still one of my friends, mentors, and heroes to this day. As a kid, I would ask him questions, and he answered them all as if he had nothing else to do. He was the one that kept the Davis Queen Fleet fishing boats running. Even at 1:30 in the morning when we were getting ready to leave on a 2 a.m. trip, he would be at the dock working on the boat with some stupid young teenager following him around asking him questions. That makes it three generations of Holley's that have captained boats for the Davis's family of businesses. My grandfather ran the Queen of Queen, one of the first Davis boats, for George W. Davis (Joe Ed, and Grover's dad) who died about the time as I was born.

The oil fields turned out to be very eye opening, and were different than anything I had imagined. Much of the work in the oil fields was not that much fun. You had to go when they said, even when the weather was bad. I was often working with people that were not very nice, because even though I worked for Marine Transportation Services, we were working for an oil company who had a company man on the rig and a dispatcher on land that gave us our daily marching orders. But it did give me a whole new experience in life. I saw, up close and personal, how the oil fields worked. We often took people to oil rigs when the weather was too bad for them to go by helicopter. That was our primary job, taking people and equipment to the rigs. This gave me hours and hours to talk to the men that worked out on the oil rigs about their jobs. There were always two captains on board, so we could technically and legally run twenty-four hours a day, if needed. One captain would drive the boat out to the rig, and the other captain would drive it back. This gave me the opportunity to sometimes have the ride out or the ride in to talk about work on the oil rigs with the passengers or sub-contractors; I gained a great education on (predominantly natural gas) oil well drilling. Oil or natural gas drilling was different than I had often seen described on TV and in the media. We often had long hours, and we were fed well; the drilling rig would even send down meals on occasion. We had a couple of rig bosses during my time there that were very nice and invited me up to tour the rig. What an operation: running twenty-four hours a day, drilling operations, safety operations, and the logistics of feeding that many people 24/7. The drilling crews worked twelve hours a day for seven days, and then were off seven days. We were on call 24/7, but worked a fourteen day on, fourteen day off schedule. The grocery box that we took out once a week filled most of the back deck of the 127' boat deck.

We worked close to the Mexican border in South Texas for most of my time in the oil field. My first oil rig to run to was in block 755; the government issued oil leases to drill in blocks. We docked in Port Aransas close to the mouth of the Corpus Christi ship channel. I thought, I really do need to learn to speak Spanish. How true that turned out to be. I still deeply regret not learning to speak Spanish, and it is one of my goals. Another of my lasting memories of working in the oil field is working on the back deck of the boat when everyone at the dock said President Reagan had been shot. We all spent the rest of the afternoon watching TV. Little did I know that I would one day meet President Reagan.

In the early 1980s, cutbacks were occurring in the oil field. I was not very happy anyway, so when the downturn occurred in the oil field, and the oil company I worked for was cutting back, I decided it was time to make a change. I had a number of people urging me to go into a variety of businesses, including sales or running private yachts. At the time, ferrying private yachts did not pay very well, fun—yes, good money—no. So I decided that if I was going to make a change, I was going for more money making opportunities, and this meant sales. I picked up a newspaper and there it was in the help wanted section, a car sales position at Tommy Thomas Chevrolet in Panama City Florida. Little did I know how drastically answering this help wanted ad would alter my life's course.

"Courage is being scared to death... and saddling up anyway."

— John Wayne

2

FROM SHIP TO SHOWROOM FLOOR

Well, there I stood on April 22, 1982… all I wanted to be in life up to this point was a boat captain, now I was applying for a job to be, yes, a car salesman. I went from the bridge, as the Captain of an oil field crew boat, to the showroom of the most well know car dealership in our town. Upon my arrival at Tommy Thomas Chevrolet in Panama City, I met with a man by the name of Joe Flumerfelt; he was the General Sales Manager. I completed a job application, spoke to him for a few minutes, and took a psychological profile test. While I was waiting on the test results, and to speak to someone else, I saw a friend of the family who was working there, Pat Brookins. She was one of the few female car salespeople in the United States at that time and a true pioneer in the field. Pat was a great salesperson, very friendly, very pleasant, and very helpful.

As it turns out, I scored very high on the psychological profile test, showing that I was a natural-born salesperson; not a very reliable test I might add, with further proof to come. I then went on to interview with the General Manager of the dealership; he was Tommy Thomas's son-in-law, Bill Cramer. He would turn out to be one of the smartest men I've ever met in life; and my interactions with him would be instrumental to my career in the coming years.

The interview with Bill went well, but I needed to meet with Tommy Thomas to complete the interview process. Sounds simple enough, right? However, L. E. "Tommy" Thomas was an icon in this part of the country. He was on TV all the time, at many high profile events, head or former the head of the Republican party of Florida, and personal friends with President Ronald Reagan. He gave cars, money, and resources to just about anybody that needed it, or that is the way it seemed to me. I had met him once or twice at the DCT/DECA annual breakfast called "the Busby breakfast" (at which I would be a keynote speaker in the future). So having an interview with Tommy Thomas was exciting but, I have to say, it was downright scary. As a matter of fact, I was nervous at almost every meeting I had with Tommy Thomas over the course of the next fifteen years; sort of like the schoolboy in the principal's office. I do not remember if the interview occurred the same day or the next day, but it went very well. For almost an hour, we talked about everything except for the car business. At the end of the interview, he said he had a retired Air Force cook working for him who went by "Dago" (whose real name was Thomas V. Delatorre). He said if an Air Force cook can be number one in the southeast selling cars, surely an ex-football player and local boat captain could make a living at it.

I was hired on the spot. They gave me books, brochures, videotapes, and cassettes to study. However, they were very busy, and I was asked to "help watch the front" that very day. On my first day, I waited on someone that my father knew and sold my first car. I made as much money as I would've made in five days as a boat captain. Needless to say, I was hooked. To my surprise, going to work at a car dealership was as much fun as it had been working on the boats. It was upbeat, a great work environment, and everyone was very kind to me, especially Joe Flumerfelt and Pat Brookins. They taught me how to meet, greet, shake hands, and properly ask someone's name and write it down. Pat even taught me how to look someone in the eye and smile with a firm handshake all at one time. Sounds simple enough, but think about who in your career actually taught you how to do these things.

The next few years I made a good living selling cars and learning. Joe, Bill, and a host of other salespeople and managers that I worked with were always pointing out ways for me to improve, or a different selling technique to try. Joe and Bill were more like professors than bosses, and they were excellent teachers. Without being in a formal learning environment, I learned more in that short period of time than I could have ever imagined. I learned about computers (as primitive as they were), inventory, and even ordering cars. In my eagerness to learn, I was assigned or ask to do a whole assortment of tasks that no one else wanted to do: locating new cars that people were interested in but were not in our inventory; calling other dealers to trade cars from other dealers' inventory (remember, no computers, we received a weekly log of all the inventory in our zone and it was very tedious to read); arranging convertibles, cars, and trucks for use in various parades also seemed to have fallen on me. I was also asked to represent the dealership at various functions when others could not attend. I must say, Tommy Thomas was so great at including his employees in every event. He invited us to many events and introduced us to anyone he knew that we came in contact with; a talent or trait I would struggle to acquire in my future role as a business leader. It was like being back on the boats again. I was interacting with people: business people from Chevrolet Motor Division, General Motors (GM), General Motors Acceptance Corporation (GMAC), well known car dealers, entrepreneurs, politicians, and local dignitaries. They all taught me something about business, life, or people. I found myself in a job that was so much fun, very different than my boating experience, but just as much fun. The people I worked with were great people, entertaining to be around, and very good at what they did. Being around and interacting with Tommy Thomas for those fifteen years was a blessing that I so underestimated while I was experiencing it.

In the writing and review to this book, I reached out to the man that hired and helped train me in the automobile retail sales business to ask for his thoughts. I wanted to test his memory of my early days in the car business to paint a better picture of how I was or what people might have saw in me in those very early years. Here is Joe Flumerfelt's response to my request: "You knew Michael Holley was special the first time you met him. His smile lit up the room, not a false or secret smile but a puppy dog smile, a genuine smile reflecting confidence and kindness. The smile inspired instant trust. The smile is rarely seen in one so young. We all truly liked Michael. The smile really lead the way to getting to know the person. Some of us would use an old Southern axiom in explaining Michael: *He was raised right.* Michael has touched on his younger years in this book. Michael's traits in relation to his rise in the retail auto industry were his winning way, the ability to have you feel comfortable with him, the willingness to work hard and be loyal. Tommy Thomas saw some of himself in Michael. I saw some of the traits I missed in myself. If I would have chosen one person to work with running a dealership, it would have been Michael. Managing an automobile dealership is a very challenging career. Lots of people equate success with sales, but profitability is the key. That means managing the parts department, the used car lot, the service department, and the body shop, all in a manner that assures success. The dealership also has a business office that pulls all the numbers together. Don't misunderstand me, sales are always the driving force, but without excellence in all departments, life can be very difficult. Tommy Thomas was a fine man, and I valued the time I personally spent in his organization. Politics in General Motors has a direct relationship to your success as a dealer. Tommy excelled in this area. Michael and I are both fortunate to have learned from Tommy. Accounting and planning for profitability was an area of Tommy's business we were not exposed to. There is so much to know that thinking any one dealership can singularly prepare you for all business scenarios is grossly unfair.

Michael would have to develop an understanding of some of these concepts on his own. Michael's time at the Panama City dealership was further enhanced by the presence of Bill Creamer, Tommy's son-in-law and dealer in residence. Bill's education and unique background helped expose us to intelligence and organized thinking. This background may have shown areas in Michael's career that led to his difficulties when the economy turned down. Lack of a great personal fortune to fall back on in difficult times is another huge factor in Michael's failures. Michael, I hope this will be of help to you and your audience in better understanding the Michael Holley of young."

During those early years of selling cars, Mr. Thomas hired a UPS driver, James Barber. He was past president of the Panama City Jaycees (the largest chapter in the United States at the time), and he was voted president of the year for the United States Jaycees. Mr. Thomas had attended the awards banquets where James was awarded one of his many local, state, and/or national Jaycee awards. Immediately after witnessing the many accomplishments of James as a civic leader, Mr. Thomas started trying to hire him. After much effort on Mr. Thomas's part, James was hired. James immediately went to the top of the board in sales and was an instant success. By the way, he scored terribly on the psychological profile exam as a salesman. After a few years of selling cars, he would get his own dealership that Mr. Thomas purchased and partnered with James. It was a Chevrolet dealership in Madison North Carolina where he would become a part of the community; his wife, Linda, would become his top salesperson. James was and is a close friend and mentor in my life. He was a man that I leaned heavily on after I became a dealer and civic leader myself. His counsel was always insightful and full of wisdom, and I should have valued it more than I did.

Selling cars was boundless for me and most enjoyable. I used it as a tool or a platform to reach out and grow personally and as a future business person. I was very immature for my age, always cracking the joke and trying to entertain. I used this time to hone, to some degree, what I had learned, acquired, or grasped while working on the boats: the ability to read people. If you love being around people, car sales is a great job because, above all else, it is a people business. Everyone I worked with or sold a car to was teaching me something. I had a good memory and remembered most of the lessons verbatim. Pat Brookins taught me how to shake hands, smile, and look someone in the eyes. Tom Dilatory taught me that keeping up with someone you have encountered or sold to previously is a must for a lifetime in sales.

I had been in the car business about 90 days, maybe 120, when I decided that I wanted to own a franchise car dealership one day, preferably a Chevrolet dealership. You know, be the car dealer, the leader, the boss that attended all the functions and was looked up to as a leader in the community; even though I only had a vague idea what that meant at the time. I'm not sure if I was being brave, naïve, or just stupid. I bounced into Tommy Thomas's office; he was sitting at his assistant's desk signing papers, and he looked up and said, "Yes Michael?" I replied, "Mr. T. I'm going to be a car dealer one day." He put down the papers he was holding, looked up at me, and said, "Son, I believe you. I hope we get to do it together, but regardless, go after your dreams, work hard, and learn all you can learn and it will happen." A man of his experience and stature could've blown-me-out or blown-me-up, yelled at me for breaking in unannounced, and made me feel like an idiot, instead he made me believe. I knew after that encounter that it was possible. How would you react if put in the same circumstance? I have asked myself that question hundreds of times.

From that day forward, I abandoned studying how to be a great car salesman, which would cause me some hard times in the future, and I began to study and become a student of the car business. It must've been something I was destined to do, because it often seemed that my two immediate bosses, Bill Cramer and Joe Flumerfelt, along with James Barber, and many other managers I worked with were my constant teachers or professors. The managers that helped and taught me were not limited to just them, though. Over the years, many would be coaches, mentors, and trainers; often without even knowing it. Within the first couple of years, I came to know Mr. Thomas's comptroller, Mr. Russell. He was a pretty crusty guy, but very smart. The dealership was still on manual accounting, which meant no computers. Many will not remember the long ledgers that they kept the accounting books on. When I would encounter him, I would ask questions. He would not allow my questioning to get very in depth, and I got the feeling that I would not learn much from him as long as we were in front of others. I knew that Mr. Russell went to work very early, so one day I went in about 3:30 in the morning and sat in the showroom. Yes, they gave us keys to the showroom on the first day, and a car to drive too. Wow! As he walked in and saw me sitting there he asked, "What are you doing here?" I told him I had some questions for him, but he was always so busy during the day; besides, I heard he liked coffee. He didn't say anything; he just started walking towards his office. He was almost out of sight when he looked back and said, "Well make yourself useful and go make some coffee." Our friendship would last until his death. He taught me about bookkeeping, accounting, and business in general. I felt like I was getting a degree. I do not remember if, before his death, I told him how much he and his lessons meant to me.

Another such person that I would meet in those early years of my business career was a young Certified Public Accountant by the name of Roch (pronounced Rock) D'Aoust, a French Canadian born in Canada but educated in the United States. He was with a firm that represented Mr. Thomas on a number of tax issues and served as his primary CPA firm. Roch would help me out of a tax jam in my early twenties when I handed him a shoe box full of W-2's, receipts, and other items from my boating days. He did a great job for very little money, as I did not have any money. He would become one of my closest friends and confidants, which to this day is ongoing and building even with all we have been through together. He was and is my personal and business CPA, but most importantly he is my friend. As with my relationship with James, if I had listened more or ask for help sooner, I might still be climbing the ladder of success. But was that my destiny?

If you are a young up-and-coming entrepreneur, salesperson, or business person, remember this if you remember nothing else from this book: Everyone is a professor, everyone you interact with is teaching you something; in some cases it maybe what not to do. The bigger lesson here is that it's just as important to learn what not to do as it is to learn what to do, and to use those experiences to build relationships with those you trust and respect. You must learn from everyone you meet that is willing to teach. Everything in life, good or bad, is a lesson you can learn from if you appreciate it for what it is.

I was very fortunate in my days of sales to have received a great education, partly due to my willingness to participate and partly due to my youth. I was sent to just about every class that Chevrolet, General Motors, GMAC, or anyone else we were associated with offered. I bet I spent a month each year in class. My pay was based on 100% commission, and I was not paid to go to school. This often created financial stress that almost caused me to make stupid decisions more than a dozen times. But it was my willingness to learn, and my friend James Barber's wisdom, that kept me from doing something stupid. This brought about my first promotion. As I said earlier in this chapter, the dealership was still on manual bookkeeping; i.e. no computers. Bill Cramer convinced Tommy Thomas to convert the dealerships to a computer system. Unbeknownst to me, Bill Cramer had asked Mr. Thomas to make me the company's first computer systems administrator. So as a barely-high-school graduate, and a mediocre salesperson, I was now the company's computer systems administrator. Over the course of the next year, I converted several of Mr. Thomas's dealerships to computer systems. This would be invaluable in the future, because doing this job taught me an awareness of the parts and service department of the dealerships, and took my knowledge of accounting to a higher level. It also allowed me to interact with the managers of different departments in different dealerships and, quite frankly, looking back, they were all very good and way above average in their fields. For example, Billie Donn was the service manager back then. He started at the dealership in his teens and is currently, as of this book going to press, Vice President and Fix Operations Director (over parts, service, and body shop) of that dealership in Panama City and another teacher in my life. For years, I called on his advice for my own fixed operations problems.

One result of all of this diverse learning and activity I was having in my short career was that I cultivated a relationship with a lot of people that did a lot of different things, both directly and indirectly related to running a car dealership. One thing I did that I think was very unique, at least for my age, is that anyone that I met or came in contact with that impressed me, or that I thought I might have some chemistry with, I wrote down their name and/or collected their business card. I would then have their information to contact them in the future if I needed something in their line of work. I also got in the habit of contacting people, even if I did not need their help, just to stay in touch. This is what started my long relationship with so many people who worked for Chevrolet, General Motors, and GMAC. I would never have acquired my own business had it not been for the relationships that I built with these people during this time; many of which are among my ongoing friends. It was also during this time that, due to the involvement of Tommy Thomas and his encouragement, I started attending events that might be out of my comfort zone. I participated in a walk-around competition testing product knowledge and sales techniques by a panel of judges, and came in as runner up champion for the south-east region for Chevrolet. I became charitably, civically, and politically active, often attending events with or for Tommy Thomas.

It was also during this time frame that my friend, James Barber, introduced me to the Jaycees. Even with all the aforementioned education and sales training, I don't think there's anything I could have done to get a better basis for managing people or public relations than the Jaycees. James even paid my dues for the first few years. As the chairman of many high profile projects, some national award winners, I learned that if you can manage a couple hundred volunteers then managing a couple dozen paid employees is easy. I also learned it is much easier to get someone to do something when you do it with them, and you both share a common goal, than it is to just tell them to do it. Jaycees and their training taught me the beginning lessons of leadership; it is much easier to lead by example and common courtesy than it is to just bark orders. I began public speaking on behalf of the Jaycees, which is something I have been very comfortable doing since then, and I owe it to their teaching. Some of these lessons I would forget and have to relearn the hard way later in life.

As I juggled being active in the Jaycees, selling cars, setting up and helping with the computer systems, organizing the dealership's involvement in parades and other events, I received a hard lesson in business. A slight slowdown occurred in the car industry, which happens every few years. Since the computers were up and running, Mr. Thomas wanted me to return to selling cars full time. He stated that there were no other manager positions open at this time, and no one was taking care of my customer base. I considered this a demotion and somewhat regretted not taking one of the other jobs that I had been offered in the computer-related fields during the course of my computer duties. My friend, James Barber, said, "You will be bored out of your mind after ninety days of doing nothing but working on computers outside of the car business; you will be so ready to get back in the car business." So, even though I interpreted my job change to be a demotion, I did something beyond my years of wisdom. I wrote a thank you note to Mr. Thomas and Mr. Cramer thanking them for the opportunity

I had been given, and telling them that I looked forward to a promotion to management when the opportunity arose. I am sure I had given it way more thought than they had. I never really heard what Bill Cramer or Mr. Thomas thought about my letter, but I did receive, as a result of returning to my good attitude and doing what was needed, the next promotion that came along. That promotion would result in my packing up and moving away from the town that I had called home for twenty-six years. All I knew about the town I moved to was that it was the state headquarters for the Florida Jaycees, the winter home of the Detroit Tigers, and corporate headquarters to Publix Supermarkets: Lakeland, Florida.

"Courage is not the absence of fear—it's inspiring others to move beyond it."

— Nelson Mandela

3

SMALL TOWN BOY
BECOMES BIG TOWN MANAGER

In August of 1987, friends and family packed up a U-Haul truck, and I waved goodbye to my few belongings as the driver drove the truck to Lakeland, Florida. I jumped on an airplane and flew to St. Petersburg Florida where my sister had moved to. I spent the weekend with my sister, Sally, and her husband, Dennis. I then drove to Lakeland Florida and prepared to start a new career that would lead to places I could have only dreamed of. Mr. Thomas had bought the Chevrolet dealership in Lakeland Florida. I would be New Car Sales Manager and help with the transition of the purchase. We were operating on a management agreement, and the purchase was not yet complete. For about sixty days, we operated under the old dealer's license and business. In October of 1987, T. Thomas Chevrolet opened for business, and I was a full-fledged sales manager, with all the good and some of the bad the goes along with that. One side note, I did it all on faith, as I had not a penny to my name and had no idea what the pay plan would be or what amount of money I would be making. I had only known the man I would directly work under for a few months when he was the comptroller of the Panama City dealership for a short time, but I had faith and trust in Mr. Thomas.

I was divorced and had been for several years, Single and in a strange town, all I had to do was work. The dealership in Panama City where I had worked for five and a half years had very little employee turnover and a very experienced management team. This was a completely different experience, a whole new learning experience. Mr. Thomas was what was known as an absentee dealer, this meant that Chevrolet recognized he would not always be at the dealership. It was quite different because, although I knew the general manager, I did not know anyone else. But I loved Lakeland from the first day I stepped foot in it. I had lived in and grown up in a small town, Lynn Haven, Florida. But the city of Lakeland was more populated than all of Bay County in North Florida. Although Lynn Haven was a great place to grow up, it lacked a lot of things that bigger cities had. Lakeland is between Tampa and Orlando, or as I tell people "forty-five minutes from Mickey Mouse and forty-five minutes to the Gulf of Mexico." I had never even attended a professional sporting event, and now had more to do in an hour and a half drive than I ever knew existed. I thought *this is going to be great.*

During the next few months, I learned as much about "what not to do" as I did about "what to do." The dealership Mr. Thomas purchased had a lot of issues and a whole lot of employee turnover. I tried to just focus on my job of selling and ordering new Chevrolet cars, but it seemed like there was so much more to do. In Panama City, I had always done so many more things that were not related to my job title. I just did them and my managers in Panama City seemed to always appreciate that I was doing them. Now, that seemed like it might be frowned upon. When my general manager was in a meeting or other events that took him out of the dealership, I was asked to make decisions or help with issues that were really above my pay grade. But, again, it was a chance to learn and get a little outside the box of my normal duties.

In late 1987, I was asked to attend a Chevrolet advertising group meeting in Tampa Florida that my boss was unable to attend.

Here I would meet another person that would become a lifelong friend, Cody Lowery. He would take me to my first professional sporting event, a Tampa Bay Buccaneers game, and he became the godfather to the son I thought I would never have. Cody is one of the most unique and entertaining men I have ever met in my life. He owned the advertising agency that the Chevrolet dealer group in Tampa used to cover the Tampa ADI (Area of Dominant Influence). I would end up over the years traveling, vacationing, and socializing with him, his wife, Phyllis, and their children. Cody would become one of my closest friends and closest business confidants. He would also be a connection and conduit for so many other special relationships that I would develop over the next twenty-five years. Cody taught me one of the best lessons in life, and until this book I doubt he knew it. Without even realizing he was doing it, he had the ability to seamlessly blend his leadership and management style with social mingling and entertaining, all while learning from those around him at the same time. The only way to do this, and be genuine, is to truly care for those you are surrounding yourself with, and to effortlessly blend all of the above. Cody would teach me another very hard and painful lesson of life in the future.

The car business in 1987 and 1988 was pretty good. Business continued to grow despite a lot of growing pains and employee turnover, including general managers. The dealership's general managers were my immediate bosses, and I had four in three years. They were good guys, people I personally liked, but they just never meshed with Mr. Thomas's organization or Mr. Thomas. At a rapid pace, I continued to learn everything I could. I was also exposed to many other things that larger cities offer, and I had never seen growing up. Besides professional football, there was baseball, as in spring training in Florida. It was also in Lakeland in 1988 that I met my future wife, Michelle Oxford. And in 1989, I would get married for the second time. Mr. Thomas saw an article in the paper about her being salesperson of the month at another dealership and said we needed a good female salesperson. He wanted me to hire her, and I did. After we were married, he said, "I told you to hire her, not to marry her." This marriage would establish a series of relationships that would result in a ninety-degree turn in my career path. Her father was a corporate controller in the automobile business, and in fact, had been the controller at the Lakeland dealership I was working at years before Mr. Thomas owned it.

It was also during this time, through a series of circumstances, that I met someone else that would become a lifelong friend and business confidant, Derrick Kelley. He was a used car dealer just starting up in Auburndale, Florida. He had lost his father at a young age. He started his own business with no money, just hard work and car sense. In time, he took that small car lot and built it into an empire of multiple businesses that are still growing. We taught each other a lot in our early days together, and he is still teaching me and coming to my rescue. He likes to say that I helped him get started, but that is way overstated. He needed to buy cars, and I needed to move some old cars and trucks, some that did not run. He took them all and sold them.

In 1988, I would meet a German lady, by the name of Gerda Goins, who had to be one of the smartest automotive comptrollers, if not people, in the United States. She would become my next professor through this journey in the business world. There are many people that I can credit with the successes that I had in business, and Gerda would have to be in the top five. She was more than smart, she made me better, and she made me better without having to beat me down to do it. She knew dealership accounting as good as anyone. Not to bore you with the details, but a franchise dealership's financial statements track the profit or loss of each department within the dealership, almost as independent businesses, and then brings them together on one page to show the company as a whole; and because of the prices of automobiles, the numbers are really big. There are many people that are very smart with accounting and numbers that really just never get the rapid cash flow and sheer amount of dollars flowing through a franchise automotive dealership, and at the pace at which that happens.

The years 1988 and 1989 were pretty much a blur. I worked for three general managers from 1987 to 1989. I got promoted to general sales manager and got married. The dealership continued to have issues, and I was very frustrated with the turnover of my bosses. In my youth and arrogance, I believed I was more qualified for the job than those I had worked for. I, of course, was not, especially in my lack of maturity. However, I would soon get the opportunity to prove what I knew, and to learn how much I didn't. All at the same time but in a different place.

Upon the hiring of the fourth general manager in three and a half years, I was very upset that I had been passed over for the job. I could see that many of the underlying issues of the dealership had not been addressed and therefore were not being corrected. Each general manager I worked for brought something new to the table and, of course, each had talents that I learned. Several of them are my friends, in spite of them not working out in Mr. Thomas's organization. It was not their fault they were brought in over me, they probably did not even know I wanted the job.

I grew to established a relationship with my father-in-law, Dan Oxford, who was the comptroller of a chain of dealerships in northern New Jersey and a brilliant comptroller in his own right. I had dinner one night in Marco Island, Florida with the owner of the chain of car dealerships that my father-in-law worked for, Jim Salerno. During that dinner, he said he was trying to buy a dealership in a small town, and if they got it they were going to make my father-in-law the dealer. They wanted to know if I would be interested in being the sales/general manager. I could not imagine a southern boy who had rarely ventured north of the Mason-Dixon Line living in New Jersey. Wow, what a ride this was to be.

But after a series of events that I was very unhappy with, and after I was told that the Salerno group had purchased the dealership in Newton, New Jersey, I knew I had some decisions to make.

I believed, right or wrong, and maybe even justly, that I was looked at as a child within the organization I had grown up in and would probably never get a chance to be "the guy". With this thought process, I decided to leave the Thomas organization and the mentor I had hoped to work for until I became a dealer. In the summer of 1990, I again packed-up and moved, this time to New Jersey. Once again, just as I had done in 1987, I made a leap of faith, without knowing a pay plan or an income. My wife at the time, Michelle, was going with me to be the office manager at the dealership. I took the job with the Salerno * Duane Group as general/sales manager of Salerno * Duane Pontiac Buick GMC Subaru dealership in Newton, New Jersey. Oh my Goodness, was I in for a learning curve.

"When you are finished changing, you're finished."

— Benjamin Franklin

4

A GENERAL MANAGER IN A STRANGE PLACE

n June 1990, having just built a new home in Lakeland, Michelle and I packed up and moved our belongings to Newton, a small town in northwest New Jersey not far from where Pennsylvania, upstate New York, and New Jersey intersect. The dealership was in some type of receivership and certain things had to be accomplished before the purchase could be finalized. The Salerno * Duane group had taken over and were operating the dealership on what is called a management agreement. This was not the same as what I had walked into in Lakeland three years earlier, but similar, meaning the problems were different but running a dealership or business under the rules of a management agreement were very similar. Running a dealership that was on a management agreement and in receivership taught me some disciplines that were very useful. The purchase was a little adversarial. There was the onsite owner who was the managing dealer, and the co-owner who was the financial backer and investor; and they were not seeing eye to eye on the selling of the dealership. To say that we were trying to sell cars and get some things done while walking on egg shells is an understatement.

I was in a new environment, with new bosses, and running a dealership under what was not the best of circumstances. But all

these things are life's learning experiences if we let them be, and
it was the perfect situation to use the knowledge I had acquired, or
thought I had, and learn what I did not know; all from the perspective of a different group of people in an entirely different environment. I had spent my short career working, studying, and learning
the ways of the Tommy Thomas organization in a Chevrolet dealership. Now was a chance to see how someone else did it, and I had
four different franchises to work with and learn how to sell their
products: Pontiac, Buick, GMC and Subaru. It was a very successful
group to learn from, and I was most grateful for the opportunity.

Since I had moved to Lakeland, I had been accustomed to working six and seven days a week, twelve hours a day or more. That was
just the norm for the car business in central and south Florida.
Here, everyone worked shift work and only five days a week. I did
what I had always prepared for, and that was to work whenever
the dealership was open. Although living in New Jersey was a major adjustment, after the purchase was complete and the group I
worked for were now the owners, we assembled our own management and sales team, most of whom had worked at the dealership
before. The new folks were me, my wife, my father-in-law as the
dealer, his wife, and my mother-in-law. A manager by the name of
Neils came in from one of the other Salerno Duane group dealerships as fixed-operations manager, which was manager of the
parts and service departments. He could and would do anything
he was asked. He was there when the service department opened
and when it closed. We became friends but I have since lost track
of him. We had a great team, and he was a huge part of it. It was
a great group, there were only about twenty or so employees, and
they were very good at what they did. I enjoyed working with them
all, even though, in life's journey, I was not to be there that long.

After my first minor snow storm, and seeing how much work it
was to get the dealership open, this Florida boy decided to rewrite
the procedures of getting the dealership operational after a snow
storm, also known as "the snow plan." Yes, a Florida kid who had

never seen more than a half an inch of snow in his life before now, rewrote "the snow plan." My idea was if we could be the first dealership to open on a snow day, we would sell more vehicles than anyone else. In the town and county we were in, seventy-five percent of the working population left town to go to work every day; on snow days many did not commute. I drew my plan out on a white board in the conference room and brought in those of us that were to execute it. The employees thought I was nuts; I probably was. But through hard work, more than I had planned, we opened quickly and sold cars. The day of good car sales far outweighed all the hard work. We implemented the snow plan several more times, and each time it resulted in good sales. For me, back then, everything was about how to sell one more car or truck, new or used, than we were capable of. It did not matter if that extra unit was the fiftieth or the three-hundred and fiftieth. This philosophy would follow me through my automotive career. I have said this in every chapter in this book: I learned quickly that it was nice to see a different way of doing things. I was not that fond of living in New Jersey, but the people I worked with, the people I worked for, and the learning experience, were magnificent, and I have fond memories of them all.

One funny story that I have to tell about myself is about a Super Bowl party in January 1992. We invited over some of the employees from the dealership, as we had few friends outside of work. I cooked for about a dozen folks to watch the Super Bowl. I had prepared a number of coolers, half filled with ice, for those that brought their own drinks. As people started arriving, they all started setting their assortment of drinks and beers on the back deck. I said, "Hey, why aren't you using the coolers on the back deck?" With much laughter, all my guests informed me that it was much colder on the back deck than in the coolers. Another sign of a transplanted Florida boy in New Jersey in the winter time.

While in New Jersey, I essentially worked for three different bosses that were each so unique and so smart. Most people would've run from the situation; but again, I looked at it as having three professors. My father-in-law, Dan Oxford, who was the onsite dealer, was a brilliant controller and retained his corporate comptroller duties. He looked at things differently than I, and in time we both communicated with each other about how to run the dealership. He, like Gerda before him, continued to enhance my understanding and knowledge of dealership accounting. Chip Duane, one of the other partners who had been one the youngest executives at Pontiac Motor Division and left the corporate world for a private ownership/partnership with Jim Salerno, was said to be very tough to work for. Maybe he was, but I never saw it. He was brilliant, tough, but fair. When I asked him a question I got a straight answer, and I learned something from every encounter. The senior partner, founder of the business, and President of the chain of dealerships, was Jim Salerno. He was a dealer that I always aspired to be like. He was smart, hard-working, stylish, and very determined in his success. I have to say, I don't think I ever lived up to being the dealer that he was or is. I could not have become the business man I became without the twenty months that I spent working for the Salerno * Duane group. They made me better and taught me a different way of both running a dealership and looking at a business model. It was a new perspective I could not have received anywhere else.

During my twenty months in New Jersey, we worked a lot, but spent most Sundays in New York City, since car dealerships could not be open in New Jersey on Sundays. Michelle's college roommate, Dianne, lived on Staten Island where she had grown up. We would often drive there and then take the Staten Island Ferry to Manhattan just to walk around, as we did not have much money. I visited, experienced, and dined in New York City and the surrounding boroughs; things a small town boy never experienced before. To this day, my favorite pizza place, Denino's Pizzeria, is on Staten Island; it has been in business since 1937. I often felt like Gomer Pyle floating around New York City, all the while learning to run and manage a multi-franchise dealership in upstate New Jersey. Sshazam!

During the latter part of my stay in New Jersey, the first Gulf War broke out and was carried live on CNN. This was not good for business... I do not recall it being that tough on us in New Jersey, but I was getting numerous reports that it did hit my former Lakeland dealership very hard. There were numerous issues, and Mr. Thomas was not happy. I called him one day and told him I missed Florida, and if there was ever an opportunity I would be interested in talking to him about returning. During our conversation, we talked about people we knew and just sort of caught up. In the end, he stated that he appreciated the call, but did not offer a hint of things to come. He, of course, knew that I still spoke to my friend and his partner, James Barber, in North Carolina frequently.

One day in late January 1992, I received a call from the fleet manager, Bill Sangster, at T. Thomas Chevrolet in Lakeland, Florida. He told me that Mr. Thomas had let the general manager go, or he had resigned, and that if I was interested in coming back to Florida I should call Mr. Thomas as soon as possible. I called my friend James Barber in North Carolina and asked his opinion; he recommended that I make the call. I then called the comptroller, Gerda Goins, and she said things were not good and also recommended that I make the call. I made the call.

"Do not judge me by my successes, judge me by how many times I fell down and got back up again."

— Nelson Mandela

5

THE OPPORTUNITY OF A LIFETIME

I flew into the Tampa airport one evening at the end of January or first of February 1992. Mr. Thomas was to return to Lakeland that day. He asked that I not let anybody know that I was coming to town, and to not contact anyone in Lakeland or at the dealership. I arrived at the same hotel he was staying at, and met with him at 7 a.m. the next morning. To say I was nervous is the understatement of the year. Some people get butterflies in their stomach when they are nervous, I think I had sea gulls flying around in there. I was scared to death. Mr. Thomas had always made me nervous, but this time I was an outsider, not the fair-haired boy that had grown up in his organization. I took with me a couple of financial statements, some customer satisfaction reports from GM and Subaru, a few letters from customers, a few other incidental reports, as well as a few paycheck stubs.

We did the normal particulars, catching up on family and friends as well as other people at the dealerships, and then… very slowly and very methodical, he started going through the reports I had brought; he did not say a word while he was doing this. I'm sure that it did not last more than five or ten minutes, but it seemed like hours. He looked up and said, "You've done a good job since you have been gone. I'm sure they're happy to have you." Knowing that they had been very good to me, the thought swept over me that I thought they were happy to have me, but I missed Florida, and I missed Chevrolet.

He told me that things were not good; the dealership was strapped for cash, and neither Chevrolet nor GMAC, our primary creditor, were happy with the operation. Customer satisfaction was not good and credit line audits had been sloppy. He said it was not going to be easy, and there would be a lot of hard work involved in fixing the problems, as well as a number of key personnel positions that had to be changed. He looked me dead in the eye and said, "Can you fix this?" I replied, "Yes sir, I can and I will." He told me, "Whatever short comings or lack of business experience you might have, hard work was not one of them." He said he knew I would do what it took to get it fixed and what I lacked in business experience I made up for in work ethic. We went over a number of other issues, and he asked what I was making, so I showed him my paycheck stubs. I have absolutely no recall what I was making or what the pay stub showed I was making. I was not driven by money, but by the performance of myself and others. I have told many people that my ego and self-worth were driven by the net profit of the company, and if that was where it should be then I was fine. He then said that if I did what I was supposed to do and the dealership's profit was what it should be, that I should not have any problem making much more than I ever had. He then said "Let's go to the dealership and see some of your old friends."

We drove to the dealership separately, and he called the remaining management team together. Several of them already knew I was in town. He had to have told them, because I had not told anyone outside of family and James Barber in North Carolina. This was before everyone had a cell phone, and texting and social media did not yet exist, so news did not travel as fast. I walked around the front end of the dealership and spoke to a number of people that I knew; they all asked if I was coming back. At this point in time, I was not certain. Mr. Thomas had not offered me the job, and other than what I was already making, we had not discussed salary. We spoke to Gerda Goins; I was so happy she was still there through all the turmoil. As always, she was very direct, and asked if we had made a deal. Tommy did not answer the question, but said, "Let's go meet with the managers." After Tommy reiterated a number of the obvious problem, he announced that I was the new general manager, without ever formally offering me the job; if you knew Mr. Thomas that was not that big of a surprise. He then said I would be there on Monday. No one in New Jersey knew where I was or what I was doing other than Michelle and my father-in-law, so there was no way I could be there on Monday. I did not want to get in this discussion in front of managers, so I let it go and we had a round of discussion, questions, and comments. I only remember saying, "Keep the wheels on until I get back."

Afterward, I went into a meeting with Mr. Thomas and Gerda, and told them there was no way I could be there on Monday, that I felt obligated to give at least two weeks' notice. He said that was fine, he understood and appreciated my loyalty, but if they didn't accept a two weeks' notice to get on the first airplane back to Florida.

I returned to New Jersey that night, spoke to Michelle, and said I was ready to go home. I then told my father-in-law, the dealer, and my immediate boss. He said I needed to see Mr. Salerno and tell him what's going on. The following day, I went to the Pontiac dealership in Randolph, NJ where Mr. Salerno's office was and waited on him to arrive. I told him that I was going to return to Florida to take the general manager's job at T. Thomas Chevrolet. It was what I had always wanted, and if things worked out and I performed well, Mr. Thomas had offered me a buy-in to the dealership. Mr. Salerno stated that they had been happy with my work and that they also had plans for me. I said, although I have very much enjoyed working with Mr. Salerno, Mr. Dewayne, and Mr. Oxford, it was time I returned to Florida, and that I really missed running a Chevrolet dealership. He was his usual gentlemanly self. He wished me well and ask when I would be leaving.

I do not remember much about the remaining two weeks, but to the best of my memory I did serve out a two week notice. During my two weeks' notice, I flew to Florida and rented a room at a bed-and-breakfast in Lakeland to stay in while the tenants renting our house found somewhere else to live. By this time, Diane, my wife's college roommate, was living with us and wanted to make a change, so she was going to come to Florida with Michelle in about ninety days. I took Diane's T-top Firebird and headed to Florida. I have told this story many times but, once I crossed the Mason Dixon Line while driving south down I-95, I bought a Budweiser and gave a big rebel yell. The story may not have been exactly true as I told it, but what was true was that I was coming back to Florida, this country boy was almost home. It was strange that since I had only left Panama City in 1987, and this was just the beginning of 1992, I considered Lakeland as my home. But as I stated, I had loved Lakeland since the day I stepped foot in it, with the winter home of the Detroit Tigers, beautiful weather, lots of fresh and salt water nearby to play in, and a great location. Although, I do regret that I never went to a Yankees, Mets, Jets, or Giants game while living in New Jersey.

In February 1992, I began a new career, and I thought that I had made it. How little did I know it was just the beginning of a journey that would take me places, introduce me to people and experiences I could not have understood because my dreams were not big enough to envision what was about to happen.

"Never confuse Motion with Action."

— Benjamin Franklin, Autobiography of Benjamin Franklin

6

THE GROWTH TO EXECUTIVE MANAGER

During the eighteen hour drive to Lakeland, I had time to reflect on the challenges that I faced at T. Thomas Chevrolet. This helped me to be prepared to walk into a tough situation, a situation that I felt like I had trained my entire adult life for. I was confident, but nervous. First and foremost, my responsibility was to sell cars or oversee the selling of new and used cars and trucks. I had been training for that since 1982. Cutting expenses would go hand in hand with building sales. In Newton, we had been able to accomplish a lot with little capital. Sales were needed, but it was just as important to make a profit from those sales. I will take more net profit with less sales over more sales and less profit anytime. Although this philosophy, while correct, would get blurry in my future years.

It had literally been just under ten years since I went from boat captain to General Manager and soon Executive Manager. We would soon become one of the top 100 Chevrolet dealerships in the United States. My new office was about ten feet from the office I had left twenty months before. I told many people I had moved a thousand miles and back just to move ten feet and have the job I had envisioned since I was twenty-one years old. I checked in to my bed-and-breakfast on Sunday afternoon. At the ripe age of thirty-one, I was ready to get to work.

Early on the morning of February 17, 1992 it was time to begin practicing what I had learned. As I drove south down Highway 98 to the dealership, the huge American flag sitting atop a hundred foot flag poll was flapping in the breeze, all of Mr. Thomas's dealerships flew this flag with the Marine Corps emblem at its base. I felt all warm inside, proud to be working under this flag. At the dealership, I spent most of the morning greeting employees and customers, reacquainting myself with who was there. Although I had been gone for just under twenty months, there had been a lot of personnel changes over that time. A couple dozen people were the same, including most of the office, and many in the parts, service, and body shop. But so many in the sales department had changed. I called a sales meeting and then a managers' meeting, and then it was time to go to work.

I have to say that, except for a couple of contemptuous meetings with the GMAC branch manager and the Chevrolet zone manager, the transition went very well. I simply told everyone we had to do it better and cleaner than everybody else so as not to be judged by the mistakes or missteps of the past. I did not want, nor did we have the time or inclination to dwell on what had been. We simply had to build on today and move forward. I was the fifth general manager in five years; both Chevrolet and GMAC were in a show-me not a tell-me mode. I clearly understood that the dealership's operational problems were causing the area managers of both Chevrolet and GMAC problems with their superiors. We had obligations to do certain things correctly that had not previously been done. They needed the problems solved and for the dealership to perform. I needed to keep both Chevrolet and GMAC happy, as it did make things easier when the relationship was good and was a time consuming distraction when it was not. My true obligation and highest priority was to Mr. Thomas, my boss, mentor, and the majority stock holder in the company I now ran. His daughter,

Ginger, was the minority stock holder and deserved no less than a reasonable return on her investment. They were the investors, and we would give them a return on that investment, plain and simple: deeds not words, positive actions not excuses. This was not going to be easy, but it was absolutely beyond a shadow of a doubt going to happen.

We were profitable in February. Yes! My first month back, and for the first month in a long time, the dealership was profitable; in the black as we used to say. We took off like a rocket ship, things went so right so fast that it was almost incomprehensible. By year's end, we were on our way to becoming one of the most profitable Chevrolet dealerships in the United States. Within a year, we had one of the highest returns of net profit as a percent of sales of any dealership in the United States. That year went by so fast that I don't even know what happened to it. Over the course of the next three years, we broke record after record of sales and profits. In late 1992 or early 1993, the Chevrolet zone manager told Mr. Thomas that since he was again an absentee dealer he would need an executive manager. I was seeing him less and less, although we talked every day, seven days a week, 365 days a year. In a meeting while he was in town, Mr. Thomas asked Gerda if she thought we had found an executive manager. She said she thought we had. He then appointed me to the position or title "Executive Manager." For this position, you go through the same approval process as becoming a dealer or owner.

Because of my youth and inexperience, Chevrolet insisted that I go to what was then called "Dealer's Son School," now referred to as the Dealer Academy. I thought it was a complete waste of time since we were already breaking records, sales were climbing, and customer satisfaction reports were great. Showing my immaturity and arrogance, I thought I was above needing to go to school.

In February 1993, having managed the dealership for one year, I was shipped off to the Chevrolet headquarters in Warren Michigan for four weeks of Dealer's Son School. Once again, a

Florida boy in the cold. The four weeks were divided into two sessions: two weeks in February and two weeks in August. I have to say, I went kicking and screaming, but for a kid that did not attended college, it was one of the most enjoyable, educational, and eye-opening experiences in my life. The people in the class were either dealer's children, dealer's spouses, or executive managers, like myself. The schooling was very intense, and we worked very hard from 8 a.m. to 5 p.m., and then we played very hard for hours unknown. We were exposed to all of the top Chevrolet brass. It was a rewarding experience. I absorbed more knowledge than I could've guessed could fit in my brain. At that particular point in time, T. Thomas Chevrolet in Lakeland had a 5.7% net profit to dollar sales ratio, or as the industry refers to "return on sales." The industry standard back then was 1 ½ to 2% net profit as a percent of sales, which is still pretty much the industry standard now. The dealer accounting instructor was a South African man by the name of Jeff. When polling the room about profit percentages, he got to our number of a 5.7% return and asked if I could walk up to the podium. I was embarrassed and a little bit confused; he handed me his pointer and said, "You can do the class because I can't teach them how to do that." I never heard much about how Tommy felt about the school, but I was told he got a call from a couple of my instructors that said, in spite of the fact of not wanting to be there, I had been a very good student with a great attitude.

While at school, I was invited, along with a lot of Chevrolet management, to attend a party at my friend, Dave Hansen's house. Dave and I met at one of the events I had attended with Mr. Thomas in the middle eighties in Birmingham, Alabama, and was one of the people I had been keeping up with. When we met Dave, he was the Chief Engineer of Chevrolet, but moved through several positions during our friendship. Through promotion after promotion. we kept in touch as Dave climbed the corporate ladder. Dave and I still visit often and remain friends. He retired as General Manager of Fleet and Commercial of General Motors and now lives in the

West Palm Beach area of Florida. I visit him and his wife when I'm in south Florida.

During the party, I was like a kid in a candy store, bouncing from executive to executive, talking about my love for Chevrolet Motor Division. I am still amazed at how attached a person can become to a brand such as Chevrolet; I know I was. It was truly rewarding to be traveling in the circles of those who ran what I believe to be one of the greatest brands in American history. I will never forget a national convention when someone said, "They don't write songs about Volvo's." I thought that was so cute. I still bleed Chevrolet blue bow ties after all these years, and want to give my thanks to Dave Hansen for exposing me to so much of it. From suite passes at NASCAR races to using me as a sounding board on upcoming projects and ideas, wow what a ride it was turning out to be.

It was also along this time in my learning curve that I was rapidly becoming exposed to the unique fraternity of Chevrolet dealers, as well as other dealership owners. People that live in a community, particularly a smaller community, have seen the activities and generosity of local franchise car dealers. Well let me tell you something—I learned, and I hope I was able to pass on to those that would in time come up under me, all the things these local business men and women do that no one knows about. Sure, you see their names on baseball uniforms and in football stadiums, but the real charity comes when the local pastor or Salvation Army Captain calls and says they need this for this and it just happens. Dealers could not be all things to all people, but I was quickly learning they did more than most could imagine.

I wish I could give more insight about my management style to those that are up-and-coming in the business world; I simply went a million miles an hour, all the time; at times to the detriment of my family and friends. As I said, I was very close to my mom, dad, and sister, but did not see them for periods of time during this part of my career. But that was the only way I knew how to work, and simply the way that I was. I often worked well over a hundred hours a week, then would spend countless hours at home combing over financial statements, Chevrolet customer satisfaction reports, and inventory reports. Some days I arrived to work at 4 a.m. or staying until midnight. It just seems there was always something to do. But those hours did not affect my energy. One day someone was looking for me, and a salesman named Frank Meredith, now another longtime friend, told them, "Stand in the corner of the showroom, and he will be by in a few minutes." Frank was correct; in a couple of minutes I came zooming by, and they caught me. I always walked very fast everywhere I went. Frank said that they needed to put a cow bell on me to hear me coming. Energy breeds energy, laziness breeds laziness, and a fast-paced work environment brings even the slowest up a little bit. I am often reminded of the saying, "a rising tide raises all boats," and unless they are sunk and sitting on the bottom they will rise with the tide or sit on the bottom. I think people feed off energy, and what I lacked in knowledge, I made up for in energy and hard work. Work hard—play hard—work harder; it worked, but it does have its price. I never saw children in my future. Wow, would that change!

I have to tell you a story: As I mentioned in a previous chapter, when watching the news coverage of Ronald Reagan getting shot in Washington DC, I had no idea what the future held for me. On Tuesday, November 9, 1993, at the Reagan Presidential Library in Semi Valley, CA, President Reagan would give General Colin Powell the Freedom award. They said it was Powell's first public appearance since retiring as the Chairman of the Joint Chief of Staff. I was there, along with James Barber, Bob Taylor, a fellow Chevrolet dealer in Florida, the surviving members of Tommy Thomas's Marine Bomber Crew (they had survived two shoot downs in WWII), and our wives, all hosted by Tommy Thomas. Tommy was a longtime friend of Ronald Reagan and a major contributor to the Reagan Presidential Library. After the ceremony, we had a private audience with the former President for about twenty minutes; he told stories and we all laughed. Afterwards, we headed back to the hotel to prepare for an even bigger highlight, a gala the Reagan's threw at a restaurant in Beverly Hills in honor of General and Mrs. Powell. We stayed at the Four Seasons Hotel in Beverly Hills (Wow, I knew I wasn't in Kansas anymore.) The gala was a blast, it was a who's who throughout the room, excluding me of course. Being an unknown did not stop me from having the time of my life. Johnny Mathis was the entertainment, and I had a number of conversations with people I could have only dreamt of meeting, like Delores and Bob Hope. I spoke to them for about fifteen minutes. I also had a conversation with Tom Selleck, and a number of others stars. One couple I spent some time talking to was Adolf Coors and his wife. I was a beer drinker and wanted a beer, but I was not sure if it was appropriate at such an event. The Coors certainly made me feel better about that. When Mrs. Coors heard me ask the bartender for a beer, she told them I would have a Coors and then introduced herself. She then ask where I was from; I replied Florida. I have a southern accent, and she insisted that people from Florida do not talk like that. I asked her how many people she knew that were born Floridians? She said, "At this, point I'm thinking one." At the end of the night as we were leaving, the paparazzi were everywhere. I did not even know what a paparazzi was.

The years after the Dealer Academy (1994, 1995, and 1996) went by at a lightning pace. I cannot tell you everything that happened in that time, for it went by in the blink of an eye. The one thing that was becoming quite evident during this time, especially during 1996, was that my marriage was failing. I worked way too much, stayed away too much, and simply was not at home enough. In the failure of my marriage, the responsibility lies with me, as my company and my business came first. Not many people would want to live under those conditions.

As I previously stated, many people that were helping or advising me on this writing project wanted me to share some insight as to my management style and work habits. First, that is very difficult for me to articulate, as I truly do not know the reason for my seemingly uncapped successes at that time, and as this book will factually lay out, I was not immune to the pitfalls that many successful people suffer. I worked hard. I always tried to be fair. I made decisions in a timely manner and, for the most part, I was almost always at work. We had very good people that were capable of accomplishing much. I truly did care deeply for many of the employees, customers, and others that supported our rapidly expanding organization.

I did have the ability to have month end close outs or month end promotions that were successful beyond expectations, often creating sales or profit results beyond forecast by a large margin, sometimes in the closing days or hours of a month. Many of the managers were very talented with auto industry knowledge, and talents above my own. Several of them had energy that was far beyond the normal person. Again, this was energy, motivation, and work ethic more than it was a skill set. I looked at every deal that was not happening, spoke to customers, and covered all departments daily to see what was going on all the time to find out how I could help achieve more, particularly at the end of the month. You truly do observe a lot, and are in the know, when you are there from open to close. I was and am a student of the business side all the time: analyzing financial statements, inventory reports, and sales reports, as well as reading every trade publication I could get my hands on. I continued the habit of calling friends and business associates to see how they were doing and what was going on. Prior to access to the internet, getting information was not as easy, you truly had to seek out what you wanted to know and learn—I did. I did not have one spare minute in any day those first couple of years. I worked eighteen hour days and then would often take the managers out afterward, meet a friend or business associate, or attend an event. I did not need much sleep and could easily function well on four hours of sleep a night for long stretches of time.

I am not sure what the lesson is here, it is what I did. If you believe it or dream it, you can achieve it: move the needle past peoples beliefs, if you will. If you have the knowledge, skill sets, and work ethic needed to do the job, then you can make it happen. Or put another way, "What the mind can conceive, and the heart believes, you can achieve." People will naturally follow a leader if you are leading with all the above. If you do not have the knowledge and work ethic, you probably will not have the respect of your people, or at least to the degree that you need to have them accomplish 120% of what is capable. Almost everyone can be risen to a higher level with good leadership and motivation. You must make them believe they can do it, and they must believe you can help. My years of studying financial statements and dealership accounting was helping as I was able to do much of my own financial analysis. Gerda did not need my help, as her knowledge far exceeded mine, but I could do a lot of my own research and come to my own conclusions about how to improve the net profit, all the while being the primary cheerleader for the sales departments.

What happened next was the biggest upset of my young business career and greatest personal loss of my adult life. What was about to happen was so unexpected on both a personal and business level. Other than losing my grandparents this would be the biggest shock in my life.

September 16, 1996, L.E. "Tommy" Thomas passed away after having open-heart surgery. He survived the operation for a number of hours, but there were many complications due to his long bout with diabetes, and the possible outcomes were not good. He passed away around two in the morning. My friend, James Barber, who was in Panama City, called me with the news. I wanted to be in Panama City, around the friends and family in Tommy's organization. The closest deaths I had experienced at this point in my life were that of my grandparents. Tommy's death was a blow, and very disheartening, and I selfishly remember thinking, "What now?"

"If you tell the truth, you don't have to remember anything."

— Mark Twain

7

THE LOSS OF A MENTOR AND PURCHASE OF A BUSINESS

The morning of September 16, 1996, I went to work; never having gone back to sleep after the 2 a.m. phone call informing me of Tommy Thomas's death. I knew I needed to inform the employees of his death, but I was truly dreading this task and trying to hold my emotions together to do it. I had called Gerda at home early to tell her, but had not informed anyone else prior to arriving at the dealership that I can remember. After getting as many people together in a group as we could, I informed them of Mr. Thomas's passing away during the night. This was quite a shock to many, as he had overcome a number of health problems over the last five years, including prostate cancer, and we all thought Mr. Thomas could survive anything.

I spent the remainder of the day preparing to be in Panama City for the next week and then caught the next fight from Tampa to Panama City. I slept at my dad's house, but spent the majority of the week at Mr. Thomas's house. I called him "Chief" in private settings, but always Mr. Thomas when in a public; most people just called him "Tommy." Many of his longtime friends told stories of his youth; this was so enjoyable and it helped with the pain. His funeral was one of royalty, a true statesman's funeral. The local

TV stations offered to cover it live, but the family declined. It was one of the most celebratory funerals that I have ever attended. Gen. P.X. Kelley, former commandant of the United State Marine Corps (July 1983 – June 1987) and a longtime friend of Tommy's, pinned the "Distinguished Flying Cross" medal on the lapel of Tommy's suit coat in the casket. Tommy's Marine aircrew had been awarded that medal, but Tommy had not yet received his. I have had the privilege of being around a number of the surviving Marine aircrew members since the Reagan library event, and they were truly a unique group of people. They were Marine's through and through, and conducted themselves as members of the United States Marine Corp at all times. After spending time with some of these men, it is easy to understand why that generation is called the "Greatest Generation." When General Kelley pinned the metal on Tommy, I don't think there was a dry eye in the house. The commander of the Salvation Army gave one of the most heart-felt eulogies that I have ever heard, and closed with the famous Salvation Army quote, "heart to God…hand to man, until such time as we are promoted to glory." Tommy once told me of the Salvation Army, "They do what they do because they love it and live it, and they get square pegs in square holes and round pegs in round holes quicker and cheaper than any other organization in the world." Reverend Si Mathison, a close friend of Tommy's and a local celebrity in his own right, officiated the funeral and closed with a heart wringing song. The funeral procession went from the church to the cemetery for a burial with full military honors. People lined the streets and stood by their cars, many saluting as the hearse drove by. I had huge tears rolling down my face, it was a sight to be amazed at, and I was so proud to have been associated with a man that had commanded such respect and admiration. It was one of the greatest honors of my life to have been chosen as a pallbearer for his funeral.

After the funeral was over and the reminiscing complete, I had to go back to work and face the employees and all the questions that were to come at T. Thomas Chevrolet in Lakeland. The main question being, "What was going to happen to the Lakeland store?" On my return, I did not have an answer, but I knew I only had two choices: buy it or look for a job. Certainly my preference was to own the Chevrolet dealership that I had worked so hard to build and that was so much a part of me. One problem: I had no money. Another problem: within weeks of the funeral my wife and I were getting a divorce. I actually kept it a secret for about three months, as I was afraid that Mr. Thomas's estate and trustees of the estate would not consider me a viable candidate if I was in the middle of a divorce. I will say in hindsight that my former wife never did anything to impede my purchase of the dealership, and after some dialogue we were quietly divorced. When I give talks and marriage comes up I always say that the most civil divorce is bad and they go downhill from there. We had no children, so it was only she and I involved in the process.

I did have one thing going for me; I owned 12.7% of the dealership stock. Acquiring this stock had been painful as I had bought it with my year-end bonus, meaning I did not get paid in cash but in stock, yet I was still responsible for the taxes on the year-end bonus. So the painful purchases over the last few years was about to pay dividends. I had an option on another 5%. If the estate honored that option, I would own more than 17% of the stock of the dealership that was now worth quite a bit of money, at least to me during that time in my life. I had options, but what I really wanted was to own a dealership and be a Chevrolet dealer. So what do I do now? What was the estate going to do? What was Mr. Thomas's daughter, Virginia "Ginger" Watkins, going to do? Ginger had been a partner in the dealership and owned 35% of the dealership since its inception. I had to find out what she wanted to do, and I did not know her that well at the time. We had exchanged conversations over the years, and she would call with questions on occasion, but I knew that without her cooperation I could never purchase the remaining portion of the dealership. Did she want to stay involved? Did she want to sell out, and if so at what price? More questions than answers.

While the trustees of the estate were determining a value of the dealership, lots of other things were going on. The employees, like myself, were feeling anxious about not knowing what was going to happen. We talked fairly frequently about the long future, but day-to-day I just had to keep the dealership going and making money. During my appointment as Executive Manager, I was also named the "Successor", which meant that in the event of death or incapacitation of the approved dealer, I would be the one to make the day to day decisions as far as Chevrolet was concerned. Chevrolet, as well as the zone manager and district manager, was very cooperative in my running the dealership during this time. The zone manager knew of my desire to buy the dealership; he often stated that if I could purchase the stock, my dealer approval would be no problem. He, as well as all Chevrolet people were supportive.

The estate approved the execution or offering of my option to buy 5% of additional stock if I could raise the money in a timely manner. I went to a number of banks, and even though I had no money, I had good credit and 12% of the dealership free and clear. I was successful at borrowing the money to purchase the 5% of additional stock and now owned 17.2% of T. Thomas Chevrolet in Lakeland. I thought, worst case scenario, if I don't get to purchase the dealership, I would be paid for the 17% I already owned. But worst case was not an option. My goal, and my only goal, was to own that dealership, at any cost.

The dealership was eventually valued at $6.7 million excluding real estate. I mentioned before there were three shareholders, myself, the estate, and Tommy Thomas's daughter, Ginger. I had to make two deals: one with the estate, and one with Ginger. I was awarded some minority shareholder discounts so I would not have to come up with the full $5.5 million. I started working on the total dollars needed, but with the clear understanding that I would have to settle with the estate and Ginger separately. The estate needed me to understand that in the estate's best interest, it had to pursue other buyers in the event I was unable to complete the purchase, and the assurance the asset brought full market value. This was going to be a stock sell, not an asset sell, which means the buyer is buying the stock of an existing company. The buyer accepts all liabilities that are inherent, instead of its assets only. I was willing to accept that risk, as I had been running the company for five years. While other potential buyers might be unwilling to accept those risks and insist on an asset sell. While trying to raise the money to execute the sale, I had to keep the wheels on the day-to-day operation of the dealership and keep it profitable. Rumors of the sale were rampant, and even though I didn't hear them there were probably rumors that I was going to be out of a job. I had to keep my eye on the ball, successfully run the company, and raise the money to complete the deal. Nothing to it, right?

At the end of all my negotiations with banks, friends, and anyone that would listen, I was about a million dollars short of putting the total deal together, as I had to settle with the estate and then Ginger separately but simultaneously. Since the deal did not include the land, I also had to negotiate a lease on the property. The most likely other prospective buyer was the Ferman Group out of Tampa that owned a number of dealerships and was one of the oldest, if not the oldest, GM dealerships in Florida; truly a great organization. I had been in talks with their CFO, Steve Uiterwyk, for dual purposes: providing operational information to them on behalf of the estate to consider the purchase, and planting the seed for a job if they were the ultimate buyer. I had a number of meetings with Steve for the above reasons. I can now say this, as Steve and I became and still are close friends, he scared me to death. He was smart and always a number of steps ahead of you in the thought process; he had an ability to see a business deal like few others. In the end, when I felt like I was out of options to raise an additional million dollars, I met with Steve at his office. After explaining where I was and again seeking future employment, he said, "If you want to be a Chevrolet dealer, then you need to get your whiny ass out of my office and go raise another million dollars or we are going to buy the store. So go ask everyone again, and tell the estate, GMAC, Ginger, and anyone else you're talking to that you're a million and a half short. See what they say." I cried all the way back to Lakeland, as I was just emotionally spent. I was in the middle of the deal and had just completed my divorce. I then called my GMAC contact, Tom Hamlin, (more about Tom's and my relationship later in the book), and said "I'm a million short." I could not lie to Tom, but I told him I was telling everyone I was a million and a half dollars short. We went over all the numbers again, as he and I had laid this whole grand plan of buying this dealership out on a cocktail napkin at Hooter's in South Lakeland months before. I carried a spreadsheet with me everywhere I went that showed what I had raised (borrowed money) and what I needed to raise (what I was short) with notes from conversations. Tom then said about the same thing Steve had said, "I agree, tell all the parties you need about a million and a half dollars to complete the deal. You always need more than you think. See what they say."

To make a very long and stressful story not so long, I have butterflies in my stomach just writing about it as if it were yesterday, Ginger loaned me a million dollars of the proceeds she was owed, which my friend James Barber co-signed for. James to the rescue again. GMAC loaned me another half million. In the end, I owed about a dozen sources for this deal, including the money for the 5% option I had exercised. I had begged, borrowed, and leveraged everything, but was able to buy out the estate and Tommy's daughter Ginger. The deal closed June 1997. The closings were at the GMAC office in Atlanta, and then at Ginger's house in Buckhead (Atlanta, GA). We had a celebratory lunch with the team that put the purchase together: my attorney at the time Matt Kovschak, Ginger's team, and a couple of GMAC folks, I think. Ginger was a most gracious hostess, and although a very tough business women, one of the nicest and classiest ladies I have ever met. I regret not asking her to remain a partner with me.

I do not think that I can reflect in words or show you the emotions and mental torment I went through to lose my mentor, maybe my job, go through a divorce, borrow more money than I ever knew existed, and carry the burden every day of running a company and what was going to happen to me and the rest of the employees if I was unsuccessful. The amount of advice, emotional support, and love I was getting from family, friends, employees, customers, and business associates would take another book to explain. What I went through both mentally and emotionally was a blessing and a curse. Just know this, at the time I thought it was the most stressful thing I could ever go through in life. I was wrong, as you will see in the chapters ahead. Having explained the above the best I can on how someone with no money raises roughly five million dollars to own a company and keep a job, know this... I could not have done it without the help of dozens of people. Without a doubt, there would not have been a Michael Holley Chevrolet or Holley Automotive Enterprises had it not been for Tommy Thomas, Ginger Watkins, James Barber, Gerda Goins, Tom Hamlin, and yes, Steve Uiterwyk, the CFO of what I considered the opposition at the time, and so many others. The moral support from executives of Chevrolet, General Motors, and GMAC often gave me confidence when I needed it. The estate trustees including my friend and CPA, Roch D'Aoust, and my one time mentor and teacher, Bill Creamer, were supportive but had their duties to see to the estates' fair market value. Unfortunately, through all this, in my perception, Roch had to remain on the sideline, so I had a substitute CPA for a few years, as I was concerned about involving Roch with the duties he had to the estate. Though, Roch and I would be reunited in short order, it was probably a mistake on my part to have not had him back on my team sooner. He never seemed to hold against me my temporary CPA firm substitution.

I also cannot convey what it meant to travel with, in the company of, and have unlimited access to my mentor and boss, Tommy Thomas, for fifteen years. As I stated earlier, we spoke every day

365 days a year, unless one of us was traveling or unable, and most of the time we still talked. We spoke almost every Sunday morning about almost everything, and it was much more laid back than our talks Monday through Saturday. I learned, experienced, and witnessed wisdom and knowledge from Mr. Thomas and those he surrounded himself with: from entrepreneurs, to politicians, to auto industry executives, and the employees that worked for and with him. Because of the doors he and those around him opened, I lived a life that a boy from Lynn Haven Florida could not have dreamed of: from visiting with Ronald Reagan, to accompanying the Commandant of the United States Marine Corps (as a current and retired Commandant), to the Friday parade at his residence in Washington DC, to visiting the US Capitol Hill with a US Senator, and one of the most memorable, having dinner with the surviving crewmembers of Tommy's United States Marine Air Corps crew. Tommy was an enlisted man, a gunner. These crewmen were truly people of a different era, they got things done with no regard for who received credit. A trait that future generations could definitely use.

In June 1997, I embarked on a journey that the best, most creative, and award-winning fiction writer could not have written on their best day. I started an *Alice in Wonderland* life that in ten years would take a turn that no one could predict. The purchase was completed in June, the name of the dealership was changed in July to Michael Holley Chevrolet, and in September of 1997, I met the woman of my dreams.

"It always seems impossible until it's done."

— Nelson Mandela

8

BUILDING AN EMPIRE AND FAMILY

In September 1997, I met Hope Davis Stephens through a series of circumstances that started with a fishing trip to Costa Rica arranged by my then business attorney Matt Kovschak. While Hope was not on the fishing trip or in Costa Rica, one of the four who traveled together on this trip, Fitz Strishley, would introduced us on our return. Hope was also in the process of getting divorced. I went from thinking I would never have children to eventually having three. Hope's two children from a previous marriage, Trey and Carter, two and four at the time, and later, Christopher Randall Holley.

During the coming years, we paid off over four million dollars' worth of debt that I borrowed to establish Michael Holley Chevrolet, including the money borrowed from GMAC, Ginger, and a host of other sources. Yes, the dealership totally repaid all the borrowed money for my stock option and the purchase in four years. I cannot over emphasize, nor do I want to over complicate this feat, but it was very hard and used up a large amount of cash. I hope that I have articulated well enough that I had no money, so this and every transaction you will read about in the coming chapters where paid, financed, or borrowed based on the dealerships after tax profits. We were, in fact, making record profits, but between paying taxes and paying off the aforementioned debt, we were not reserving any cash.

I then embarked on building a company, empire some would say, that even I could not comprehend. Just to give you some idea of the growth in those ten to twelve years, the full year prior to Mr. Thomas death, 1995, the Lakeland Chevrolet dealership, T. Thomas Chevrolet had roughly $27 million in annual sales and revenue. Through growth and acquisitions, in the calendar year ending December 2007, that number would top $150 million in annual sales and revenue, consisting of five franchises (Chevrolet, Kia, Pontiac, Buick and GMC) in three dealerships at three locations, in two cities. We also owned an independent used car lot and numerous real estate holding companies. That may sound glamorous, but it was not. With my ability to do a deal or complete the acquisitions, there was a certain degree of self-satisfaction; however, the amount of management needed to operate all these businesses was growing even faster. I understand that it was pretty amazing to those watching it happen, as many thought I was doing it effortlessly. With this rapid expansion came rapidly growing payroll expenses and rising debt. I was never that concerned with the debt. If I could net the 1% to 2% return on the sales that I mentioned was the industry standard, after all the expenses, including the interest expense from my acquisition's debt, I was ok with that. It was said, and it's true, I became immune to debt risk.

During this time of rapid growth, I would acquire two more dealerships, and an empty Kmart building. The Kmart building was adjacent to the dealership property, in fact the dealership property wrapped around the back of the old Kmart building. Kmart had built a new building and had moved on. The property had been several businesses, and ended up sitting empty for a while. I negotiated buying the property with the building owner, not Kmart, for several years. We finally came together on the numbers. I was negotiating through their in-house agent. After we agreed to the dollar amount, I then informed the agent I had no money. He said,

"You have negotiated on this for two years and have no money to buy it?" I said, "That's right." He hung up, and a few minutes later the owner called and laughingly said, "Wow! We have a deal, and you have no money." Yep, that is correct. He held a note for me for several years, and was paid. You never know if you don't ask.

I would go on to be a member, board member, or officer on innumerable boards, including some that, to this day, are still near and dear to my heart. The work of the Salvation Army and its advisory board hold a special place in my heart. I joined, or was elected to the Florida Automobile Dealers Association Board of Directors as a district director; served on the local and national advertising boards for Chevrolet, helping to decide how advertising, marketing, and promotional money would be spent; as well as working on various charities, political campaigns, and other boards. I did and do believe strongly in political, charitable, and local civic involvement; and I strongly believe we need more business people active in politics and with local charities. Small businesses can move mountains when they try to.

It was sometime in the mid-90s that I would be asked to co-host a talk show on a local AM radio station: WLKF 1430. That did not last long. After the station was sold to Hall Communication, I would be asked back to host my own show—an automotive talks show called Bumper to Bumper. I so enjoyed those years on the air of giving advice and taking calls from those trying to get a better deal or find out what might be wrong with their car. The experience in the studio would be invaluable as I would go on to do more public speaking, write, and produce my own television and radio commercials, as well as be a guest on other shows during this time, both for myself and the political and charity events I was ultimately involved with.

September 11, 2001, I was in Washington, D.C. for the NADA/ DEAC annual political conference. The National Automobile Dealers Association political action committee (DEAC) would bring together a group of dealers for briefings on current political activity and actions affecting the franchise automobile dealers and their respective state Dealers Associations from around the United States. We would then go to Capitol Hill and meet with members of Congress and their staff to discuss current legislative projects. Some time on September 11, 2001, I was to have met with my local Congressman after he returned from Florida aboard Air Force One later that day. Needless to say events took a dramatic turn for all of us. That morning, we were in briefings for our day on Capitol Hill in the convention center at the Grand Hyatt, just blocks from the Capitol. There were a number of political dignitaries in the convention center, some were meeting with their local dealer delegations, and some were scheduled to speak. It quickly became evident that the events happening in New York were not the only concern. Soon, all the political dignitaries were escorted from the building by Capitol Police and taken away by police escort. We received word of the jet hitting the Pentagon, and some said they heard the explosion and saw the smoke. The rumors then started spreading that there might be more jets heading for the Capital, the White House, and other points in Washington D.C.

Chaos was hitting the streets as thousands of staffers were sent out, more like ran out, of buildings in and around the Capital, as well as the Congressional offices, and onto the streets of Washington D.C.—many without their purses, brief cases, or even shoes. My friend, Steve West, saw a staffer from his hometown and gave her money for the subway to get home; she was not wearing shoes and did not have her purse.

A number of us started discussing how we could get out of Washington D.C. At first, we were unaware of the grounding of all aircraft and the closing of airports. A number of us started calling people we knew with airplanes to see if we could get picked up since commercial traffic was shut down. We were informed that all airspace and all airports were closed. The hotel then told us we could stay as long as we needed, obviously no one would be checking in. My wife, who was at home with our two year old baby, told me to get my suitcase and get out of the city even if I had to walk. My friend from Knoxville, Tennessee, Steve West, spoke to his son, Charles West, who was in Knoxville, and he rapidly started calling dealerships for a car. Somewhere around one to two o'clock, at a dealership in Washington D.C., Charles located a vehicle we could buy, a Chevrolet Suburban. Part of the Tennessee delegation and I were able to proceed in a gray-market taxicab to the dealership to buy the Suburban. By this time, the only things in the air were Blackhawk helicopters and U.S. Air Force fighter jets protecting Washington D.C. We were successful at picking up the Suburban that Charles West had secured for us, and we started making our way out of Washington. To the best I can remember, it was somewhere around 5 o'clock before we actually got out of Washington D.C. and started traveling towards Tennessee. The plan was to drive with my friend and the other Tennessee dealers to Maryville, just outside of Knoxville, and stay with Steve West for the night. On the ride to Tennessee, at approximately 6 p.m., we saw Air Force One overhead returning to Washington with fighter escort. During the ride to Knoxville, I gave a number of interviews, via cell phone, to local newspapers and radio stations in Florida as to my observations of the events I witnessed in Washington D.C., and the amount of panic that had built as a result of events and of all the rumors. We arrived at Steve's house outside Knoxville just after midnight.

The following day I arose early. I was very anxious to get home to my wife, family, and employees. I drove to West Chevrolet in Alco, Tennessee, just south of Knoxville, and picked up a vehicle. While leaving town, I saw the strangest sight at the Knoxville International Airport, there were airplanes and commercial jets of all sizes, from all airlines, parked on every square inch of the tarmac and taxiways. They had hurriedly parked all the grounded aircraft wherever they could since the airspace above had been closed. I then proceeded south, headed to Lakeland via I-75 through the heart of Atlanta; traffic was very light, and no one ever says that about traffic in Atlanta. I stopped at a Cracker Barrel just south of Atlanta for a quick lunch, and the place was only about a third occupied. In listening to the radio on the drive home, it was very evident that our lives had changed forever. I arrived in Lakeland at 6:30 p.m. Needless to say I was glad to be home.

The coming years were filled with growth, board meetings, and watching children grow up very rapidly. I was Chairman of the Florida Automobile Dealers Association (FADA) for the 2004–2005 term; this was one the fastest years of my life. FADA's headquarters is in Tallahassee Florida, and I spent a lot of time there. I traveled to Tallahassee almost every week during the Florida Legislative Session, which is held every year in March and April. The FADA staff in Tallahassee was small, with just three full time employees in the office: Amy, Mandy, and the Association Executive, Ted Smith. They were an army when it came to getting association business done. They treated me like family and always kept me on task; they made me look good. I so enjoyed my time with the association and the friendships that arose from serving. Lobbying on behalf of my fellow Florida dealers and business people became a passion. During the years surrounding my time as Chairman, I also served as State Chairman of the National Automobile Dealers Association Political Action Committee DEAC. My duties were fund raising, helping select business friendly candidates to support for U.S. Congress, and getting them elected or helping them stay in office. I was honored as State Chairman of the Year out of the fifty-six or so other State Chairmen, and was humbled by the recognition. At the time, I did not fully appreciate the amount of time and resources it required to divide myself between my rapidly growing companies, FADA, DEAC, and the many boards and political events for which I was working. I credit my assistant, Katie Decker, as the secret to keeping it all together and making me look much smarter and more organized than I was. She had a talent that was so unique in the business, political, and charitable world that I was participating in, and that was dealing with the various staff of the boards, politicians, and charities, as well as dealership employees and customers. She did this with the greatest of ease and made everyone feel good. She and her husband, Eric, are close friends that I am in regular contact with. I must also commend my wife, Hope, for her patience, understanding, and support during this very busy time. I can only imagine the burden my traveling and working so much put on her and the family. She helped with many charity events, as well as the many political fundraisers we supported. A friend of mine once said, "Hope could organize an event for 200 people easier than most could make a reservation at a restaurant."

As I mentioned, Chevrolet dealers, the franchised dealer body as a whole, do a lot in a community; more than most people will ever know, and for that I am proud. I'm very proud of the many things we did for others. One of the greatest projects ever started as a joint venture with Chevrolet, the local Chevrolet dealers, and Major League Baseball was Chevy Youth Baseball. The dealership and I had been very supportive of local youth baseball; you know, hot dogs, apple pie and Chevrolet, and yes baseball. It had first started in Atlanta with Chevrolet and the Atlanta Braves. An executive with Chevrolet, Tim Hudgens, wanted Tampa, along with the Tampa Bay Rays, to be another market to share this program. He and the Chevrolet zone manager, Jim Gurley, pitched the advertising board, and I was all in—hook, line, and sinker. I thought this was the greatest program ever for the youth of our communities, and Chevrolet was a natural to spearhead it. I also have to say that the folks we worked with at the Tampa Bay Rays were the best. They did, and do, so much for the kids involved in this program. I was so happy to hear that it survived the budget cuts of the past and is still around giving to local little leagues today. Thank you Chevrolet, Chevrolet dealers, and the Tampa Bay Rays for doing the right thing for such deserving kids and a great sport.

As time moved on we, as a family, were able to get away on some weekends to Anna Maria Island, on the west coast of Florida, where many of our friends had beach houses. We spent time on our boat, the Motor Vessel Princess Hope, that our family loved so much. Boating was truly the only way I had to relax and sort of leave the business world behind. The boating trips to the Florida Panhandle, Florida Keys, Dry Tortugas, and our favorite, the Bahamas over the years is a book in itself. I enjoyed sharing my love of the sea with the family and our many friends who accompanied us on these trips.

God loves with a great love the man whose heart is bursting with a passion for the IMPOSSIBLE.

— William Booth, Founder of the Salvation Army

9

THE BEGINNING OF THE END

Needless to say, 2008 was a very difficult year for a lot of people. It was an especially difficult one for me on many fronts. At the end of February 2008, my father was hospitalized for complications of liver disease, never to return home. We went through a very difficult six months with him in and out of a coma, in and out of ICU, and in and out of short rehab stints (always returning to the hospital). I spent eight to twelve hours a day with my father, and I am glad I did. I would do it again, and I think anyone with a severely ill relative or loved one would do the same if they could. It is almost as if the very sick need a referee and a coach to sort out all the many things going on between the many specialists and caregivers involved. I cannot say enough about the staff of the hospital where my father spent most of his time, Lakeland Regional Medical Center. They truly gave it their all in a situation that they probably deemed medically hopeless. But if that was their thought, they never let us know. My wife, Hope, my sister, Sally, and I are very thankful for how they treated us and my dad. It was very difficult losing my father and my best friend, but watching him take the final walk of faith, to be promoted to glory, was rewarding on many levels and helped so much with the pain. Then to hear the stories of all the people he had touched in his life gave us comfort. In his day, my father was one of the winningest Peewee Football (ages eight to ten) coaches in the U.S., going on to retire after ten years of coaching with a record of 110 – 12. Just three years prior to my dad's illness, his wife, Betty, had lost a battle to ovarian cancer. It had been a tough couple of years for my dad. Needless to say, from February, when he entered the hospital, until his funeral in July, was a very trying time. It did not prepare me for what lay ahead...

One of my managers, Kim Gonzales, reminded me at a later date that in November 2007 I held a managers meeting stating, "I did not have a good feeling about 2008." I do not remember saying that, but he is very confident in his memory of what I said, stating: "We needed to tighten-up and be careful." Obviously, with the time I spent at the hospital and away from the dealership(s), from February until July, I did not follow my own advice. I certainly did not do the best that I could, and did not properly oversee the "tightening-up."

Upon returning to a more consistent work schedule in July, business was slowing down. The automobile industry is very cyclical, down cycles every few years are not uncommon. I had a new seven-million-dollar complex for the Chevrolet dealership and re-modeled the old Chevrolet dealership, which now housed the Kia dealership. I still owed a couple of years lease on the old Kia facility and opened it up as another independent used car lot. I was heavily invested in commercial, as well as personal real estate. Over the past years, Florida real estate had been a very solid investment. I had accumulated an amount of debt that I would not survive.

During the month of August, business became tougher and tougher, and car sales were decreasing across the nation at a rapid rate. My managers and I were having a very difficult time cutting costs fast enough to keep up with the declining business, and there was nothing we could do about the very large mortgage payments that were due every month (or at least, at the time, that is what I thought). In hindsight, as September rolled around, I should have sold off some of the assets before the crash, or brought in a partner to help stabilize the financial situation; if that was even possible at that point in time, since the fourth quarter of 2008 would go down as the worst financial month since the great depression. But inherently, all car-guys, including me, think they can make it better and sell their way out of any situation. When Bill Heard Chevrolet, the largest Chevrolet dealership chain in the country, at least in unit volume, filed for bankruptcy protection and closed on September 24, 2008, I was very concerned. Bill Heard Chevrolet, one of his two Chevrolet dealerships in Florida, was forty-five minutes away and was our biggest, most aggressive competition at the time. They were the only GM dealership in our market to out sell us. I thought if we could pick up enough business from their closing, that might just get us through. I was wrong.

This part of the book, from a writing perspective, is the most difficult, if not the most painful; but from my memory perspective it is the easiest. I am painfully aware of every minute, and the painful details. I can replay many conversations in my mind as if pushing the play button on a recorder. Although, July through September are mere blurs in my memory, October 1st to December of 2008 slowed down to a snail's pace. It was like watching a train wreck or car accident in slow motion. I remember the details, but cannot comprehend how things got so bad so fast, and how so many facets of our business and lives just turned ugly and dark. When discerning the question, "how did things get this bad this fast?" it might be easy for the sideline quarterback, or the backseat driver, or even for myself, to have a say on what all went wrong and what I should have done differently. People have asked why I didn't just close and go into bankruptcy like Bill Heard Chevrolet. I will say this now, and will probably say it again in this very book, I should have declared bankruptcy and put the management of the issues in the bankruptcy court's jurisdiction.

But I didn't, and that is just a fact that I will live with for the rest of my life. There are a whole host of reasons why I did not. First, in the very beginning, I still thought the business was salvageable, and it was. The press put a lot of pressure on many institutions to do things they would not have otherwise, or made them react quicker than they might have. Second, we could not be assured that the unpaid liens would be given priority treatment in court; that is now not the case. Third, I wanted to help control the transfer or transition of the company, if that was to be the outcome, so I could protect as many employees as possible; that would not happen. Fourth, I had nothing to hide. The only thing I had done that I thought might be considered wrong was move money around between entities to help keep the company afloat; something almost all small and large companies have done. I had no personal knowledge of the trade-ins that were not paid off being sold to retail customers. Fifth, I had not stolen any money. I only sold stock in a company I owned and distributed the monies from that transaction to all three companies equally. It was my money, and I had informed GMAC, my primary creditor, that I was going to do it. These reasons do not release me from the burden of leadership or fault for my decisions. They are an illustration of my thought process to give you a better insight as to my line of thinking.

My long time business attorney and friend, Tim Campbell of Clark, Campbell, Landcaster & Munson, said it was time for a bankruptcy attorney. Tim, who was not my business attorney when I purchased the dealership from the estate, had been my attorney through the years of my rapid growth and expansion. We built a great friendship while building this business that many would call an empire. We even served on a couple of boards together. Tim's counsel had served me well over the years, and I had waited too long to inform him of the issues and ask for help or advice in this circumstance.

We hired one of the oldest, most prestigious bankruptcy law firms in Florida, if not the country, Stichter, Riedel, Blain & Prosser, P.A., to represent the dealerships. Harley Riedel was the lead counsel, and would, in time, be joined by Edward Peterson, a partner in the firm. One highlight of this business failure is the friendship that Edward and I have formed. Harley had worked with Tim during the purchase of my last dealership purchase. The company/dealership I bought was in bankruptcy, and we needed some very specialized expertise to put the deal together. With all the knowledge and legal expertise the firm had, they could not assure me that all my concerns would be addressed in bankruptcy. We decided to wait and get a formal contract or offer to purchase and would use that if bankruptcy became necessary. This strategy is called a "staking horse bidder." That was not our first or second plan, but would evolve into being the primary plan.

I am not stating that Stichter, Riedel, Blain & Prosser Law Firm advised me to stay out of bankruptcy court per se. I just hope I have illustrated what my concerns were to an acceptable level. It is not my desire to sell you on agreeing with me, just for you to understand my view point at the time. It is also noteworthy that the financial crisis was still unfolding.

I will use this paragraph as an analogy. This story could be inserted into many places in the book, but I choose here, as it might help you understand my thinking. Keep in mind that every news report you see, story you read, rumor you hear, are all created by someone that is on the sideline and has the luxury of hindsight. And we all know that hindsight is 20/20 vision and expressed with great confidence, even when incorrect.

Here is an analogy you can relate to: I ask you this, does anyone know when the captain of the Titanic knew the ship was lost? I tell you that the experts now say that it was lost the minute it hit the iceberg and several bulk heads we breached. However, no one will ever know, with certainty, what was in the captain's mind and when he believed or knew the ship was lost. I can tell you that if an entrepreneur were in charge, Captain of the Titanic, they would think the ship was savable even as the deck chairs were floating around the upper deck. A business going down can resemble a ship going down, and since some sinking ships are saved, it is not too difficult to understand why the owner of a business, a lot like the captain of a ship, would be tempted to conceive that the business may be salvageable at any stage.

I have been on four vessels that could have sunk. One was a sixteen foot runabout that flipped in heavy swells; the boat was saved and all passengers were safe. The other three, one of them I was in command, could have easily been lost but were not due to experienced crew and all decisions going correctly. We used to say that it takes three mistakes to sink a ship; just don't make all three. The problem is, until it is over, you do not know what three they were. You get the idea that when it all goes right there is little to talk about or rehash. Although, in my business situation lives were not lost but many lives were adversely affected, some in dramatic ways. In the end, around 200 jobs were lost as the purchasing dealer did not keep everyone.

I have to say that my gut feelings, as wrong as they may have been, were that I needed to stay at the helm until we fixed what we could before the ship went down. Maybe that was my captain training, or maybe I was delusional. It was my perception, that at the filing of bankruptcy, everything was lost: for me, my employees, and my customers. Within the first couple of weeks of October, I had a clear plan that was well under way of being executed for making everyone except myself whole. I was going to lose everything personally, but my plan was to sell outside of bankruptcy court. Excluding the mortgage companies, everyone from the customers, to the employees, to the creditors would be made whole, at least financially. I had at least two qualified buyers with sufficient offers to do all the above, so it was not fantasy. Although I am taking great strides to take the blame for all decisions, the actions of many others deflated the price or worth of the dealership to an unacceptable level. Let us just say, I gave a lot of them the ammo to take shots across the bow until one or two shots went straight through the hull.

I need to go back to the final weeks of September. I believe, with all my heart, if I had declared bankruptcy I would have avoided the criminal issues that derailed all the plans. Also, I believe that if I had just laid it all out for the different investigation agencies, especially the state attorney's office, things would have gone differently. But that is hindsight and my perception, and may have nothing to do with what might have actually happened.

The last two weeks of September were so financially horrific that we were struggling to make payroll, and I was feverishly moving money around to keep things afloat. I had sold my dealership in Bartow Florida to the manager of the dealership. However, when the purchase would ultimately be complete was very much an unknown. I did, however, receive a substantial down payment that I thought would buy the time we needed to fix the leaks and get the ship upright. Sort of funny in hindsight, that substantial payment came back to haunt me. The down payment was supposed to be made to me and then distributed to my three companies as part of the sale agreement and verbal communications with GMAC, who had already sent me a letter that I needed more capital in the business. Instead, the money was inadvertently wired to my Chevrolet dealership. For tax reasons, I withdrew the money and then distributed it to all three dealerships per the agreement. I sold the stock personally. Later, I was accused of stealing this money. According to information provided to the clemency board investigator much later in time, someone had seen the withdrawal from the company but did not, or was unable to, see the deposits back into the companies for the same amount of money. But this was just a blip on the radar screen.

In the final weeks of September, there were some customers who traded in automobiles and whose trade-ins had not been immediately paid off. I could write an entire book on how this is possible, but how all of this works internally in a dealership is extremely complicated. However, here is an explanation of why it is not so simple to pay off a trade-in, sell it, and get money for selling it. The problem is you must have the title to make a trade-in with a lien on it legal to sell. Even in today's electronic society and banking world, there is a time lag between paying a car off and getting the title. So without going into a long dissertation, by the first of October we had fifty something vehicles without titles. Approximately twelve or fourteen of them had been paid off but had small shortages (usually a few dollars, where the pay-off amount or date was calculated incorrectly) or the titles were hung up or held for one reason or another. There were about thirty-seven cars that had not been paid off, and one or two of these had been sold, and that was a big deal. I, of course, could not know about every transaction at all the locations; and since sales were rapidly deteriorating, we were attempting to sell as many cars as we could. I was, however, aware of the unpaid trade-ins, and that they had to be our highest priority. I was aware, at some point in time, of a few cars that had been sold to retail customers without a title; although, this was after the fact, and is really no one person's fault that it happened.

On or about October 1st, my Bartow dealership (that I had already sold part of and was under contract to sell the balance) bounced a check to GMAC. It was not that dealership's fault, as all the accounting was centrally located. GMAC came in to do an audit, and we were deemed "out of trust," which pertained to cars on our credit line that were sold and not paid off, these are different than the customer trade-ins. It was also discovered in this audit that some of the unpaid trade-ins were due to GMAC. There had been a number of cars and trucks wholesaled to other dealerships and auctions that were unpaid to GMAC, but were paid off to banks on behalf of the customers. They were not due to be paid until five days after the sale, this was part of the out of trust situation, and it was also the money I thought was needed to save the dealerships and get them sold. Again, I was wrong, and in the end it would not have been near enough. It was also a huge part of what I did to alienate the folks at GMAC, some of whom had been friends for a very long time. They simply said give them the money and we would be fine, but the money was already gone to cover the overdrafts, payroll, and keep things going. Although, I will say it many times in this book, there was no way to make all parties whole without keeping things going and completing my plan to sell all or part of the dealerships quickly. That is the one thing I turned out to be correct about. When all of the aforementioned could not be paid on the spot, all notes for all dealerships and real estate companies were deemed due and payable (meaning the notes had all been called), and GMAC occupied the dealerships taking all keys including unpaid trades. They brought in an audit team. One caveat to this is in November of 2008, GMAC was broke due to the mortgage crisis. Their automotive division was sound and making money as it always did and, to my knowledge at this time, no one knew GMAC was broke; I certainly did not. So many of the people who were making decisions for GMAC at the time probably did not know themselves what was going to happen or if they would have jobs. Many of them had worked for GMAC most of their adult lives.

I had two people that I had spoken to, both of whom I was well acquainted with, that wanted to buy the dealerships (Chevrolet and Kia). I also had an additional buyer for the Bartow dealership, should that deal under contract not close. All buyers were cash buyers needing little or no financing, so the financial crisis would not impede their ability to make the deal. However, on or about October 15th, with press in tow, a multitude of government agencies served a search warrant on the dealership. By this time, I was represented by a number of business, bankruptcy, and criminal attorneys. So the attorneys did the talking, and I was simply sequestered to my office during the entire search, never being asked for my help or input as to what they were looking for. I don't remember exactly what they were looking for, as they were not soliciting much help. They were there a very long time until one of my longtime employees finally helped them get what they needed. At this point or at least when the news broke, it was no secret I was broke and the dealership was insolvent. We were just not, regrettably, in bankruptcy court yet. As I said earlier in the book, this was a mistake that I would live to regret on many levels. However it would open doors, that I never could have foreseen, and was a most regrettable way to get to where I was going.

Within days of the search warrant being served and the intense press coverage that followed, the worth of the dealership dropped about a million dollars; however, it was still worth enough money to make almost everyone whole with the sale of the dealership(s). It is beyond my comprehension why things moved so slowly, but it was partially due to the rumors of General Motors and GMAC's possible bankruptcy. Lehman Brothers had filed bankruptcy on September 15, 2008, and the news coming out of the banking world was a daily horror story. There was a looming, if not already in full stride, financial crisis. Many people I knew, regardless of the amount of wealth, money, or connections they had, did not know how bad the crisis was going to get or what banks and other financial institutions would survive. Banks had stopped loaning money, and many were on the verge of collapse or under scrutiny of the government. Banks were calling or not renewing credit lines on businesses that were not in trouble, thus putting those in trouble as almost all businesses rely on credit lines in time of trouble. In November, I had two viable letters of intent to buy the dealerships. One major requirement of both buyers was that the dealerships remain open and the core group of employees that ran the day-to-day operations remain. It became increasingly difficult to do business with the occupation of GMAC at the dealership since they had to approve every automobile transaction, wholesale or retail, but were not allowing finance deals. GMAC was in control of every sale and was paid any money they were owed first, regardless of payroll or other vendors. GMAC monitored the incoming mail and took all checks; simply stated, a GMAC representative sat with me when I opened the mail and took any money. I again question why I simply didn't give up and run to the bankruptcy court. I thought, at the time, that getting a buyer for the dealership with an ironclad contract was the best and fastest way to take care of the employees, get the unpaid trade-ins paid off, and make GMAC, as well as other parties, whole. It might have been naïve, but I believed all or most parties still could be made whole. Again, this turned out to be incorrect mostly due to unforeseen happenings that I could not be anticipated.

Through mid-December a number of trade-ins had been paid off through the help of a friend, Derrick Kelley. He had taken the risk of paying off the cars, waiting for the titles, and then picking up the cars. He paid off well over a third of the total outstanding cars; and for that, I am eternally grateful.

December turned out to be the end, instead of the beginning of the end. We were in talks with GMAC to continue funding the operation of the dealerships through the finalization of the purchase that I believed would occur in the next sixty days. But instead, on December 18, 2008, I was arrested at my office by the local state's attorney investigator. To say this was unforeseen and unpredicted was an understatement; it was a great surprise to many but especially to me, and more importantly the potential buyers and GMAC. My attorneys asked me to delay posting bail to see if they could get it lowered. I didn't have the money anyway, it was being paid by friends. They were able to get it lowered, and I was released about thirty-two hours after my arrest. However, it seemed more like a week, and was the most horrific experience of my life, to date anyway. During this time, GMAC sent all the remaining employees home and closed the dealership. There was also a pretrial release order attached to my release that was so vaguely written that it made it impossible for me to operate the dealership. One person at pretrial, I don't remember who, said that the way the pretrial order was written, I could be in the restroom and be rearrested for that not being an approved reason to be at the dealership. So my attorneys suggested that I stay away from the dealership until the order could be amended, and that took almost a month. I must say that during this entire ordeal many government agencies surprised me by their lack of understanding of the actions they took and the results for the customers and employees involved. I think that was mostly due to lack of knowledge, suspicions of my intent, the amount of time the purchase was taking, and mainly my lack of communication to them about what was happening. What I should have done was communicate a detailed explanation of what was actually happening. I also know that just as I will never understand a bureaucrat or the bureaucracy that they work in, they could not have possibly understood what I was trying to accomplish and how. I sold them short on trying to get them to see or understand the goals, how I planned to accomplish them, how long it would take, and what the alternate plans were.

I have used this analogy to explain to people the situation I was in the best way I can. When you are stuck in a pond full of alligators, there is a lot to worry about; the one alligator you have to worry about first and foremost is the one that's got a hold of your leg. At that point in time, or at least until my surprising arrest, it was GMAC I was trying to get to let go of my leg. I truly believed working with GMAC was the quickest solution to getting everyone paid, especially the unpaid trade-ins, and getting the business deal complete. Nobody was going to be happy with anything until that happened. In hindsight, I think the government agencies, particularly the state attorney's office, felt as though I was disrespecting them, had a different agenda, or did not consider them worthy of involvement. None of that was true, but now I certainly can see it from their perspective. I have to say that the intense press coverage, at least on a local level, impeded my judgment and seriously hampered the selling of the dealership, as many potential buyers were wary of the intense and inaccurate reporting. The press was reporting a lot of details, many that were just plain incorrect. The buyers outwardly said "we are not going to do this deal on the front page of the paper. GMAC, to my knowledge, was not speaking to anyone pro or con. Again, everyone's perception is different.

I know with all my heart that if I had I communicated more openly with the press, the state's attorney, as well as others there would've been a different outcome. But I don't think that's what was supposed to happen. To this day, I have a hard time understanding how, the guy who had built this huge business, could have made so many consistently bad decisions, but I did. In the beginning of 2009, with rumors circulating that General Motors was going into bankruptcy, the deal to get this wrapped up seemed to be in doubt. After my untimely arrest, the weeks out of the dealership, the closing of the dealership, the loss of all employees and inventory, we now had no choice but to proceed to bankruptcy court with the best offer we had in hand. That, in itself, resulted in a whole new set of circumstances, delays, and problems. On top of this, two more times, one with notification and one without, I would be arrested until the charges totaled ninety-nine counts. The money spent on bail and legal fees were more than enough to have paid off all the unpaid trades as a single net transaction. I guess I was just too proud to have asked for help in advance.

As we prepared to file for bankruptcy, finalized a stalking horse deal with a buyer, and continued to work on agreements with GMAC, who had now received a government bailout of $9.7 billion, things would in fact get worse. As I said earlier, bankruptcy created a whole new set of issues because the United States Trustee's office (the United States Trustee program is a component of the United States Department of Justice) was micromanaging the details of the purchase offer. I guess that's understandable considering the handling of the case by the press and the amount of time it had been going on. I still went to work every day, after the pretrial release order was amended, trying to get this mess mopped up the best I could. Understand, as I said before, that most people's frustrations were with how long it was taking. I could certainly understand their frustration since I, more than anyone, could not understand why it was taking so long, and I was the one getting beat up on a daily basis, and was an emotional wreck. I did have a few former employees that still went to the dealership when we needed help. We often worked with a generator to help prepare the documents and other items for prospective buyers, GMAC, the bankruptcy court, as well as the U.S. Trustee's office. Pat Dee's, my longtime office manager and then comptroller after Gerda's retirement, as well as a few others were invaluable during this time. Seeing them work by flashlight or generator, and for free, brought tears to my eyes; so many were like family.

Somewhere during this time I changed criminal law firms and had two close friends represent me in the criminal part of the case: Bruno DeZayes, of Cuban descent with a passion for helping others, and Bill Friel, a career policeman who chose to retire and become a lawyer, with whom our families had been friends since our children attended elementary school together.

So many of the decisions I made to this point were wrong, many more than the proverbial three wrong decisions to make the ship go down. My decision making skills seemed to be better at promoting growth and a positive atmosphere. It was now time to "get this thing over." I often speak of how hard this was on me. I can't even comprehend how hard it was on my family, from my wife, to my children, to my mom, to my mother-in-law, and everyone else who loves me. I am sure I was very little help or comfort to them. Just prior to this all starting, I had lost my father, and during that time I felt like Christopher, Trey, and Carter had lost a father and stepfather, and Hope had lost a husband. I cannot even comprehend how bad it must've been to be around me back then. The unwavering support of my family, friends, and some special guardian angels, are the only way I survived this. The year of 2009 was rough and things were moving slowly. During the summer, I took a job at a boat dealership that was owned by a friend. It was an hour drive away, and although it got my mind off things, I was never around my family except at night and on Sundays. As this job was winding down, the bankruptcy proceedings were moving along, painfully and slowly, but moving along. There were so many thousands of little hang ups and issues that the bankruptcy process alone could be a book. Then when you throw in the persecution of the press and the legal system, I truly was doing all that I could, but that was not a lot. It seemed like I spent hours upon dozens of hours fetching documents and reports that I am not sure anyone ever looked at. Plus, anything I needed from the dealership, which was most of the items requested, I had to get by using a flashlight or buy gas for the 7.5 kw generator to start up the lights and the computer system. I am still amazed to this day that I never jumped off a building as so many did during the financial crisis. For the record, I never once even considered it. You're probably thinking *no way*, but the thought of suicide truly never entered my mind. At my very lowest moment during my very worst times, of which there were about three or four per week, one of the guardian angels that I referred to above would call me. I remember one time sitting in the backyard in the swing crying and wondering how in the world can I possibly get all this done with no resources and a closed dealership, knowing that the remaining trades, about half what they were on October 15, 2008, and some other items had to get paid. About that time, one of my most faithful guardian angels, Linda Zimmerman, called and read a Bible verse to me. She always knew when to call. Within a few minutes of that call, I found the strength to get back to work as there was still much to be done. From October 2008 these repeated calls happened hundreds of times, just at the time I needed them, and they're still happening to this day. Besides Linda Zimmerman, there were dozens more that I heard from a lot: Frank Meredith, a longtime friend and employee, and Msgr. John Caulfield, our long time parish priest. I frequently met with Msgr. John Caulfield, my spiritual advisor, longtime pastor, and close friend. One thing that sticks in my mind, and helped me keep my perspective is something he told me at breakfast one day, "Only one perfect man ever walked this earth, and we know what they did to him." He took the time to point out the good I had done for the community, friends, family, church, and church run school. Like the other guardian angels, he would just call out of the blue and tell me, in his Irish accent, to meet him for breakfast or lunch or just to talk and pray. One other guardian angel is Bill Mutz, the local Ford dealer. I guess for years he had been a competitor, but it certainly never seemed that way; he was a friend. He and his wife, Pam, have the ability to pass along the Lord's Word in a very simplistic and humble way. They taught me to pray daily for myself and those around me, and to forgive those who delighted in my failures. He remains a close friend. I know there are so many special people that God has put on this earth to help others in need: Eva Stewart, Linda Zimmerman, Frank Meredith, Father Caulfield and Bill Mutz are such champions for all but there were so many more.

"While we may not be able to control all that happens to us, we can control what happens inside us."

— Benjamin Franklin

10

THE ENDING OF AN EMPIRE

After the bankruptcy court approved the sale of the dealership to a party that was a stealth buyer through much of the process, meaning a different buyer than those that had been involved, I thought it was the beginning of the end, but it was not. It was just the beginning of a whole new set of problems with a buyer who had a severe learning curve as to the complexity of the deal. I had been keeping all potential buyers in the loop as to all that was going on and what would need to be cleaned up from the sell. Since it was an asset sale, they were not acquiring or accepting any liabilities but were required to pay off the third party liens as part of the deal, one of the most important parts of the deal to me. The original deal that was presented to the court included a consulting fee to me that was intended to be a backstop in case the trade-ins (third party liens) did not get priority claim status. But the U.S. Trustee's office locked in on this provision as some sort of kickback to me. I even met, off the record, with someone from that office to explain what was going on and how it would work, and that I would never actually get the money. I would waive the provision if the court granted priority status to the third party liens. They seem to clearly understand my intent and the plan, yet walked out that room and resumed the same objections as before.

We killed a lot of time defending the consulting agreement when, in the end, it did not matter as we worked out a deal with potential buyers, GMAC, and other major creditors; and the judge approved the deal for the third party liens to be paid. It became a moot point and the consulting agreement was removed. Instead of the process speeding up after the judge approved the sale to the stealth buyer that was now public, a whole new set of issues came up. But at this point people were out of patience, understandably so, and we just needed to get this done. So the only thing I could do was help the best I could, anyway I could, to the best of my ability and with limited resources.

It seemed that everybody involved, from the government agencies to the bankruptcy court, all legal teams, the folks at GMAC/Ally, General Motors and the buyers, wanted to get this done; at least it appeared they wanted to. Then on June 1, 2009, General Motors filed for Chapter 11 reorganization or bankruptcy. The deal ran into the GM bankruptcy process and basically went on hold. At the end of this, I still faced ninety-nine misdemeanor and felony charges that needed to be addressed, all the while I had no money, no job, and a sale that had seemed so simple six months prior that at this point we weren't sure how long it would take or if was even going to happen. Again my failure to go immediately to bankruptcy court was coming back to haunt me.

In the end, it all was completed. The trade-ins were paid off, a year too late, government agencies were made whole, and the rest of the creditors were processed through the normal course of bankruptcy court, most getting almost nothing. My legal team, and I do mean a team, (Tim Campbell, my long time business attorney and friend, Harley Ridel and Edward Peterson along with many others in there firm as well as my current criminal attorneys, Bruno DeZayas and Bill Friel) was able to get a court order from the federal bankruptcy judge, Judge May, overseeing the bankruptcy to reinstate or make right any customer's credit issues caused by the delayed pay off of their trade-ins.

As a result of the Bill Heard Chevrolet and Michael Holley Chevrolet cases, many of the concerns I had have now been addressed by either the involved parties or the bankruptcy court rulings. One example is when a person purchases a car from a dealership and is trading in their existing car. If the dealership does not make the pay-off due to business failure, that person is protected from owing the balance on their trade-in. Another example is that if a customer's credit is negatively affected by loans not paid off in a timely manner by a dealership as a result of insolvency, there is now a precedent in Federal bankruptcy court to have the negative credit reporting corrected to not reflect the non-payment by the dealership.

To all those on my legal team, as well as GMAC/Ally's counsel, Chuck Tatelbaum, who had also offered advice and support for this motion, I am most grateful. I had no higher priority in this entire process than making our customers and employees whole. I am sure that did not happened, as there was no way after this debacle of a failed business that I could have made people happy or everyone whole. But we certainly did the best we could in the worst economic disaster since the great depression. We did not accomplish all I had planned, and I would lose everything material in my life and ultimately my freedom, but we did more than a lot of people thought was possible.

As I stated above, nothing seemed to happen the way, or in the time frame, that I had planned in October and November 2008. I am sure much of that was due to my own bad judgment and incorrect decisions. Even if it all went perfectly, and it did not, 275 people lost jobs, with only some of them being hired by the new owners of all the dealerships. Many of my advisors blame this on the intense local press coverage and how it made some people react, but I am not sure. There was a lot to be done. It was complicated; and in the worst financial times of several generations, many of my decisions early on complicated matters even worse. The loss to the employees, customers, and the many non-profit organizations we had supported for so many years cannot be underscored enough, not to mention the sub-contractors and suppliers we had relied on for so many years, many of whom were like family and I had known since I moved to Lakeland in 1987. I do not pretend to understand how it affected all of those people. Of all that I lost, I did retain my family and many friends. The one friend I did lose was Tom Hamlin with GMAC, to whom I owe so much. I should have trusted him and his knowledge to help. I was with him just a week or so before all this started, but felt like I was protecting him by keeping him in the dark. In the end, he could have been another guardian angel had I just had the courage to reach out to him. But I, and I alone, bear the burden of my judgment and blame for that. I lost everything material and would, in time, lose my freedom.

"Speak ill of no man, but speak all the good you know of everybody."

— Benjamin Franklin

11

CRIMINAL PROSECUTION

As I have told so many since this time, no one can take away your love of Faith, Family, and Friends. Having survived the bankruptcy, I was alive and had my faith, family and friends. In late 2009, with the conclusion of the business deals in sight and my participation in the bankruptcy process almost complete, you would've thought I could see the light at the end of the tunnel. Well that light turned out to be a train, and it ran right over me at full speed. After having completed the painful sale of all of my business assets in bankruptcy court, and overseeing paying off of the trades, as well as the court ordered correcting or repairing of the credit reports of involved customers even though it had taken way too long, I was feeling something positive about how much had been accomplished in a very difficult business environment. The fact that it took so long seemed to overshadow what had been accomplished. I am still amazed that my business attorney, Tim Campbell, and bankruptcy attorneys, Harley Riddell and Edward Peterson, supported by a host of other attorneys and paralegals, were able to accomplish what they did with the lack of resources to do it. I am forever grateful for them sticking with me, both for their legal expertise and friendship.

Now it was time to face the criminal charges. My criminal at-torneys consisted of two friends, Bruno DeZayas and Bill Friel. They sent a message that they needed to see me urgently. They let me know that the states attorney's office wanted to hear my side of the story with all the gory details. They had said they did not want to talk about "just get the mess cleaned up and the cars paid off," it was going to be on the record, and was going to be pretty tough. They were right, it was; and I still have no idea what their perception was after hearing my side. I understand that many in that office could not understand why I did not just close and go to bankruptcy court as the Bill Heard Chevrolet group had done.

I couldn't tell you if it was a day or a month when we received word that they were not going to take prison time off the table, no way no how. From what I had heard, most believed my punishment should be somewhere between hang him on the courthouse steps, to let him go since he has been through enough, or give him pro-bation since it was due to the worst of financial times. Well, they didn't hang me; my friend said that was only because they couldn't. They sure didn't offer probation correction, but they did offer one hundred years of probation—after prison. Okay, that's a slight ex-aggeration, but not by much.

Not to get too hung up on the process, but after some wran-gling and negotiations we settled on two years of state prison and a long probation that could be terminated once all conditions of the plea agreement were satisfied. The conditions were some res-titution to the court system and some of the banks involved, some other miscellaneous fees and charges, plus all third-party liens had to be paid; to my knowledge, they all were. Terminating the long probation after conditions were met turned out to be a whole dif-ferent story, though.

After verbally accepting the agreement and several weeks of back and forth working out the language, then a series of hearings that would finalize it and allow the overseeing judge to sign off on the deal, there were also a number of lingering issues with both customers and the bankruptcy court that I needed to get cleaned up.

April 8, 2010 was the day before my final hearing, and when I had to turn myself in. I must say that the day was beautiful, so I used the opportunity to take my son, Christopher Holley, fishing off Anna Maria with Capt. Matt. Christopher. He caught a fifty-pound cobia on light tackle, which took him about twenty-five minutes to land. After a day of no keeper fish, the look on his face, both after landing the fish and the folk's comments back at the dock when they saw it was, as the saying goes, priceless. My many thanks to Capt. Matt for this very special occasion. It was also a sign that through all the tragedy and suffering my family and I had endured that there would be sprinklings, and then a creek, and then a river of hope. I am not sure if you believe that God would do a miracle for a little boy on his last day with his father for twenty months, but I know with all my heart he did. That night a host of friends and family came over, and I grilled, fried, and smoked the fish that we all enjoyed so much. Oh yeah, through all this I had started cooking. I was the only Holley male in our family that did not cook, and since I had the time I started cooking my dad's recipes, then creating my own, which I am still expanding on.

On April 9, 2010, I was accompanied by many friends, my mother, and my sister as we went to the courthouse for my final hearing. As we drove into the courthouse parking lot there were TV trucks, and I knew they were here to cover my sentencing hearing. We had decided that Hope and the children would not be in the court. Even though there was a lot of grandstanding, the outcome was predetermined, and this turned out to be a correct decision, as the press was as merciless as ever and seemed willing to crush anyone's feelings for the story that they had already preordained and reran a couple of hundred times in the past years. There were a couple of delays, as well as some procedural items to be handled, and one person who wanted to speak because they were not sure that their credit had been correct was allowed to speak. I could not tell you if the hearing lasted five minutes or five hours, but at the end I was taken away out the back door and lead to a holding cell in the back of the courthouse. My life had changed forever... And not all for the bad.

I was in the county jail for less than a week. I was in solitary confinement, or protective custody, due to my case's high profile coverage. An inmate slipped a book through the chow (food) hole while on his break out of his cell (we got thirty minutes of every twenty-four hours out of the cell), it was a book about Frederick Douglass. He repeated this every day, and I think I read three books during this time. It was hard without my reading glasses, but I did the best I could to pass the time. I was so appreciative of his kindness, and I have no idea who he was.

On Wednesday April 14, 2010 about one in the morning, they started my transfer to state prison. They rounded us up, about a dozen or so of us, and one of the guards suggested that I not mention protective custody to the state corrections officers, as I would probably not like that. We were taken to book-in in Bartow Florida to be processed out of the county system. Then we boarded a van around 5 a.m. and were transported to the Central Florida Reception Center Main Unit, about twelve miles east of the Orlando International Airport, for processing. It was a very large facility of about 1600 men, not counting the work camp or the small medical camp. To say that I was scared to death and stressed to the max was the understatement of a lifetime. This was about to be the worst day of my life.

"The secret to getting ahead is getting started."

— Mark Twain

12

PRISON BLUES

W
e drove through a couple of security gates into a se-
cure location at the reception center; we were now in
the custody of the Florida Department of Corrections
(DoC). The twelve or so of us from Polk County were stripped
naked, searched, made to stand in place, then in a push up position, and then standing again for what seemed like an hour. We
were still outside, and it was still cool in the middle of April. We
were then given a pair of boxers and remained in the holding area
outside.

They asked us to listen up for our personal belongings brought
from County. I had asked Polk County officers to leave my be-
longing (what I was wearing in court) in Polk County and my wife
would pick them up, so I did not expect to have any belongings
at the DoC reception center. When they called my name, I very
timidly said "Yes sir," as I was very cold and scared. They called
again, and I held up my hand. That is when the guard hit me. I
guess I had some kind of a weird look on my face because he hit
me again. The group around me seemed to be in shock, and no
one said anything. I remember the guard as if it was yesterday.
I hold no malice towards him even though he had more criminal intent to assault me than I had ever had for a business to go

under; and here I was and there he was. The second time he hit me the other guard looked away. It did hurt and leave a couple of bruises; nevertheless, I ended up having a great deal of respect for the environment that these folks worked in. But if the point of this was to use someone as an example to the incoming group, you would have thought someone younger with a smart mouth would have worked better.

We were then taken inside and given our DC number, sort of the social security number for the department of corrections. It lasts for life. If you ever go back, you have the same number with a letter at the end; your first time is an A, then B, and so on. There were some there with an H. I was like, "Man, I've been here an hour and I get it. I ain't never coming back."

We took our property to a counter and were asked if we wanted to send them home. I said yes, as I had a pair of $600 custom shoes with special insoles bought by my insurance company for a foot problem I have, plus the shirt, pants, and belt I was wearing in court. The same officer that hit me said, "You got any money in your account?" I said that I didn't think so but my wife would take care of it if they shipped it. Again, the same officer that hit me told the officer in front of me, "Get that shit off his counter and throw it away." So the officer in front of me shrugged and tossed the bag in the corner behind him. I would later learn that they give that stuff to the inmates that are being released from that prison. We then had our heads shaved, showered in a shower of what felt like boiling water, were told to shave, and were given prison uniforms. They were tattered rags, really. There was a V-neck with a pocket, similar to scrubs, a white T-shirt, and thin, light blue, cloth pants with pockets, an elastic band, and a white stripe running up the legs. If you're driving in Florida and you see a state prison road crew, yes we still have them, this is what they will be wearing. There were inmates wearing real pants, same color, with a belt, but they were the permanent inmates that were housed and worked there. We were supposedly just passing through.

We then saw a nurse who gave us a quick glance over, but she did check our vital signs. My blood pressure (BP) was high. By this time, I had been off my blood pressure medicine for almost a week. I told the nurse this, and she said I would see a doctor the next day. The next day, I borrowed paper to start a journal for what was to become this book, though I did not write down the number in my journal.

While waiting for something, (we did a lot of hurry up and wait) I saw an inmate that was not getting dressed fast enough get beat and kicked by a different guard than the one that assaulted me. This guy had something wrong with him and was moving very slowly but they hit him anyway. They told us to face the front of the room, as there was nothing to see. Some guy said something, and the same guard that hit the other kid came over and slapped him upside the head. The say that the inspector general of DoC installed cameras in all the reception centers, but this still happens, just out of view of the cameras.

We then received about four hours of orientation before being issued bedding and bunk assignment. Our primary instructor was an inmate called "Big Mike." He was big! He must have been there a while, as several of the inmates with the G's and H's behind their DC numbers seemed to know him. He was very kind, and I asked him a few things. He answered with the true intent to help those that wished for help in entering this new and strange world.

They put me in a two man cell in a two story building. My cellmate was from Plant City, Florida, a town just west of Lakeland. He was in on drug charges and seemed to be nice and helpful. He had been there several weeks and sort of knew the ropes, and was one of the house men of the dorm, meaning the janitor. He gave me a pen, paper, and a stamp to write my wife, and told me what to tell her I needed to buy from canteen. He was the first of my many hundreds of guardian angles I would meet in this environment.

I was "called out" (a call out is an order to the inmate and permission for the guard to let you out to go to a predetermined place for a specific reason) my first night there for a blood pressure check and was told I was on two a day blood pressure checks until seeing the doctor. I said, "Aren't I seeing the doctor tomorrow?" She replied, "Yea right." I'm not sure who ordered the blood pressure checks, but they did nothing about the blood pressure results, though they did check them twice a day. The first number I wrote in my journal from 4/15/2010 was 187/115. That was very high, even for me. It was seven days before I saw the doctor. In the meantime, I still saw a nurse twice a day who kept checking my blood pressure and saying that it was high. Sometimes they would lay me on my side in sickbay; sometime for an hour or two in the dark until they would get a lower level. Then they would send me back to my bunk, still without medication; only in DoC, I guess.

One night they left me there through "count." Counts are mandatory at every prison and are busily done at the same time at every prison every few hours. They count every inmate then balance that count to the master count of the entire prison to make sure no one escaped. You have to sit on your bunk and be quite for the entire time it takes to complete the count. Sometimes this took two hours, sometimes just thirty minutes, but it was very stressful for me. It is a big deal in prison. So that night I messed up the numbers for an hour or so, but they finally found me. I was just doing what I was told, so even though the guard that found me was mad nothing came of it for me.

When I finally saw the doctor on 4/22/2010, he told me not to leave the building until I had my medication; he also discontinued my twice a day blood pressure checks. As a result of a recent CAT scan, it was determined that sometime in the past years I had two mini strokes. To use as a base, I had a CAT scan before going in the system that was normal. I am very sure the mini strokes occurred during this time, as I had a few weird things going on with my right foot but just wrote it off to stress at the time. I truly was afraid of what might happen if I complained. My rookie prisoner thinking was that if I got hit because they didn't hear my name, then I do not want to think what would happen if I complained about medical care. Plus, I thought you had to be healthy to go to work release, and that's where I thought I was heading. Wrong again!

Getting the medication was a whole new ordeal. I was in the same building where the pharmacy folks sat in a cage and you picked up your Rx. The pharmacist said, "We do not have it yet. Go back to your dorm and you will have a "call out" to come get them." I explained to her what the doctor told me, so she said to sit down and she would call me when she got it. A guard asked what I was doing sitting there, and told me that I should go back to my dorm and wait for a call out. I told him what the doctor said. He said that did not sound right to him, more or less saying I was lying, so he was about to send me back to the dorm when the pharmacy person called my name and said she had received a "stat" order for me not to leave, and she would have it ready in a minute. The word stat is a medical term and it comes from the Latin word "statim" meaning "immediately." Two words I would never hear again in the DoC system.

One more little thing, just to give you an idea of how crazy things can be and how dysfunctional an agency this size can become, we were required to leave the dorm for cleaning for a couple of hours every morning if we were there and not assigned to do something else. It is called recreational time or "rec." About half way through this couple hour time, they rounded us all up. Hundreds of men were rounded up and lined up by dorm. I had no idea what was going on, and all the repeat guys that were there said it must be a "shake down." (More on that term later.) They were going by each dorm, and when they got to mine they called my name. There must have been about fifteen of us lined up, and they let the others return to the "rec" yard. They then marched us to the medical building, and put us in a room. A female officer came in and started yelling at us about missing a call out, and told us that she was going to write us a "CC." I had no idea what that stood for. There are three write ups for disciplinary reasons, a note on a card kept in the dorm, then a "CC," then a "DR." I have no idea what they mean, but a DR will get you sent to the "box" or "jail," meaning solitary confinement with no privileges. Now in my short time there, I had been told if you get a write up you were ineligible for work release for ninety days; so I thought this was the end of the world. It seemed like everyone in there told her they did not have a call out in order to go to medical that day. But she did not believe us and started collecting name badges to write us up. My blood pleasure was through the roof. My face was red, and I was shaking. Once again, I was being accused of something I did not do and that did not happen. I was not on the call out list that day, and almost everyone in the room was saying the same thing. Now they might or might not have been lying, but I was not. So she called me in and asked me to sign the letter of reprimand, and one of the repeat inmates told me not to sign it. I was very scared as to what would happen, but in spite of thinking I was about to get a beating, I had already seen a couple in the T&R building, I refused to sign it. Then she very angrily said she was putting it through anyway and to go back to my dorm. The sergeant over our dorm was walking out as I was walking in to the dorm. She was very sharp, and I had watched her handle a number of situations in my short time there. I was boiling mad and told her what had just transpired. She knew, because she was on the "rec" yard when they rounded us all up. She took the time to walk back in and check the call out sheet. She said, "You're not on it, and there are no notes on the security log for them calling for you." The sergeant then told me to write to my classification officer, using her name in the request, to explain what happened and ask the reprimand letter "CC" be rescinded, and that she could check with the dorm sergeant to verify. Over the next couple of days, I checked with everyone I remembered from that assembled room, and all of them swore they were not on call outs that day. So I am mad, my blood pressure is through the roof because I thought that the CC just issued was the end of my chance to go to work release in a timely manner. It was months later that I received a note in response to my request to my classification officer to correct this. It only said, "No record found of the CC you referenced, matter closed." Wow! After that whole dog and pony show, involving a dozen officers rounding up hundreds of men to find fifteen or so guys on the "rec" field, just to find out they must of just trashed the CC's she had written. Folks, this kind of thing happened daily, not always involving me, but I was the fly on the wall watching it happening and writing it in my journal.

Two days after seeing the doctor and being on my meds, I got another medical call out. At 10:00 p.m. on a Saturday, they called the dorm officer for me. I was already in bed. The nurse said she had to check my blood pressure. I told her the doctor had discontinued my daily blood pressure checks. She said I had one left from the two a day order; probably from the night I saw the doctor. She checked it and it was 127/92, then said, "Wow, are you on meds?" I told her that I was, and she said that is too high, then made me lay on my side until it came down a little. Only a government agency would get you out of bed to check your blood pressure, just to check a box on a discontinued order, then do nothing about it.

Another story, as I was waiting to see the nurse one night for a call out, maybe the same night as the above, an inmate was acting weird and the guard was giving him a hard time and yelling at him. They yell all the time at the reception center. There was an older orderly I had spoken to several times before, and I mentioned to him I had seen that guy in there before and he did not seem right to me. So the orderly got the nurse; she intervened and took him to the back under the watchful eye of the guard. While picking up my meds one day, the orderly told me the inmate in question was diabetic and that he was having many issues, and thanked me for the heads up. Again, this kind of thing was not all that uncommon.

I was at the reception center for about two and a half weeks, and I cannot express with words how stressful it was. I have a lot more stories about those two and a half weeks, but there are so many details that I am reluctant to take up any more space. One highlight, the only highlight I should say, was that since no one could contact me, my attorney, Bill Friel, got an attorney visit and came to check on me. Another guardian angel had arrived on the scene at the correct time.

On May 3rd at 2:55 a.m., the door slid open, and we assumed that my bunkmate was being shipped out as he had already been there a long time, so my bunkmate was packing. You do not know anything, and they will not tell you anything. But it was my name they called to pack my stuff, which was not much, and come down to the common area and wait. Next, they took us to the chow hall for a count, a roll call, and then to eat. You will see me mention "counts" a few times as we were counted four or five times during the day and a lot more at night, maybe even hourly. Some of the counts were very stressful as we had to sit on our bunks until the "count was clear," and in the bigger institutions that could some-times take an hour or more for them to balance the count of the whole compound. After we are in bed, they just count us asleep unless they cannot see you, then they wake you up.

They held us in the day room for about forty-five minutes, then in the Sally port for about another fifteen minutes. Next, they lined us up outside in front of the canteen with the other people from the other dorms, and then we marched in line to the chow hall for roll call and count. It was now about 4:30am and there were eighty-six of us in there. I counted all kinds of stuff and wrote it down. We then had breakfast and were taken, or marched, to the T&R building, where we had arrived. The guard that hit me ap-peared to be in charge this morning, but he was not a sergeant or lieutenant, so not sure why or if he even was. He just said, "Sit there and be quite, and it will be an easy day!" We were then herded on buses in shackles and he started driving. We stopped several hundred yards away at the annex on the same property and picked up a few more people. I thought that since I was the first stop I was going to be close and that was good. From conversations with my attorneys, information from Department of Corrections, and the rumor mill (we called it inmate.com) of the experienced inmates, I had always assumed that I would either stay in Orlando or be sent to some minimum security facility until I qualified for work release, as with time served and good behavior I had less than twenty months remaining.

We left the work camp and started driving; it was a very long bus ride. It was hot and noisy with a few guys sleeping, a few guys smoking, and some just being annoying. I overheard one of the inmates we had picked up at the annex, or work camp, say that the orderly told him we were headed to Hamilton County in North Florida, and the inmate said, "That's bad, isn't it? He said, "Hell yeah."

"It is said that no one truly knows a nation until
one has been inside
its jails. A nation should not be judged by how it treats
its highest citizens, but its lowest ones."

— Nelson Mandela

13

THE PRISON SYSTEM NOT SEEN ON TV

I was sent to Hamilton Correctional in North Florida on the Georgia line. We were unloaded at the Annex, unshackled and processed in. Once again that meant being stripped, searched, and all your property gone through and searched. While searching my property, one of the officers found a picture of Christopher with his Cobia he had caught. Hope had mailed me the picture to the reception center. The guard asked how big, and I told him about fifty pounds. He said, "Big fish." He then looked at me and said, "Car dealers screw everyone." He laughed and then said, "I always wanted to say that." Then he looked me dead in the eye and said, "You used to make a lot of money, didn't you?" I just nodded and moved down the line. They then sent us to chow (lunch) and told us to report to our dorm afterward. My bunk assignment was in Delta dorm. I just crawled into my bunk and wanted to cry, maybe I did. There were about eighty men in Delta dorm, and someone told me several were from Polk County, FL. A man approached me and said who he was, and that his brother was a friend of mine and used to work for me. He told me both their names, and his brother had been a friend, although I had not seen him in a while. He said he had thirty-five days to go before he got out. He said that I would probably be shipped to the main

unit the next day, to just stay on my bunk, not interact with anyone, and wait for my transfer up to the main unit. Once again as
a beginning writer, I have no way to express with words on paper
how stressed or scare I was. The brief interaction with the prisoner, even though he was related to a former employee and friend
of mine, was no comfort, and I hardly slept that night. Hamilton
Correctional was not a minimum security facility, it was a bad and
nasty prison that would be my home for the next six months or so.

The following morning, just as the guy had said, the houseman or
laundry man called my name and said to pack my stuff because I was
being transferred to the main unit. I thought, Oh God, if you are ever
going to send me another guardian angel, now would be a great time.
We were told to stand in front of the chow hall. One of the guards
that checked my incoming group in took us back to the room where
we had arrived then took roll call. He checked our "face sheets," (a
sheet that had your picture and all your pertinent information on it to
make sure you were you). He checked our IDs and loaded us in a van
for the quick ride up to the main unit, a several hundred yard drive,
but they backed up to each other on the same property.

The sergeant that checked us in and gave us a quick camp orientation of the main unit was very nice, and that day was pretty
uneventful. I was assigned to B dorm on the main unit and given
a job of picking up cigarette butts on the recreational yard. The
job title was "wellness," which is pretty funny. Little did I know that
God had already sent me several more guardian angels. There is
so much to say about the next five months at the Hamilton facility
that it is hard to know what to include and what not to include. It
is very difficult to describe what it is like to lose your freedom and
have your every moment being control by someone else. I passed
the time by reading anything I could get my hands on, and writing
to my wife and to the others who had begun writing me. In just a
few weeks, I was receiving as many as a dozen letters a day, by far
the most in the dorm. Three people wrote or sent something every
week. Mary Ellen Self, Gene Casey and Bill Parry, may he rest in

peace. I cannot comprehend that level of disciple and caring. After being in the system for over three weeks, I was still not allowed contact with the outside world except with letters via snail mail, as phone privileges and visitation had to be approved by the new facility, and nothing in DoC moves very fast, although mine probably happened as fast as anyone's but it seemed to take forever. This seemed so cruel and so simple to correct. If someone is not barred from seeing or talking to someone via a court order, then why not let them talk to family on the phone. The calls are recorded anyway, or that is what they tell you.

I did a lot of reading, mainly borrowed books at first, then from the facility library, and then from books Hope and others ordered from Amazon and other places. People could not send books, only publishers or other such places could. There are a number of instances that I will write about to show that those of faith are guarded to accomplish their mission in life and fulfill God's plan, in spite of their own bad judgment. For every horror story that I saw while in DOC custody, there was a positive lesson learned, and some things you just have to think happened for no other purpose than humility. I was getting a doctorate in humility, and it was coming from the college of hard knocks. It is hard to tell what God's purpose is when you're in a situation like this. Many pretend to be religious when, in fact, they just use religion as a con to get something from you, but that is no reason to suspect or treat everyone that way. Those that are of faith seem to show it over time. We must assume everyone that we're interacting with is onto a new path or another part of the journey we call life, and hope that our inner wisdom and faith helps us accomplish that for both ourselves and those that we are interacting with, for however brief period of time that is.

An example of one of my guardian angels was a man who used to be a professional football player. I do not remember his name, but in my journal I called him Big John, and he was big, not fat, just tall. We would discuss his thoughts and interpretation of passages in the Bible that he had read. I really do not feel as if I was contributing that much other than just listening and interjecting some common sense analysis of his thoughts and readings, as I am far from being all knowing about theology. One day, a fight involving several people broke out in the dorm. I simply went to my bunk and sat there with my legs crossed. Guards came in from every entrance, and although I'm not sure how many guards, it seemed like dozens. As they were getting everyone separated, I just sat on my bunk and cried. One of the guards started pointing my way and yelling go to your bunk. I just sat there not knowing what to say, as I was already in my assigned bunk. As they started walking towards me, a very large hand was placed on my shoulder, and my guardian angel stood behind me and said, "Mr. Holley, I got your back. You don't need to worry, you're safe." Once everyone settled down, he slowly walked back to his bunk, just after they had threatened to cuff him and take him to "jail." Jail is what solitary confinement or "the Box" is called in prison; one of the more inhumane things they do to inmates for punishment. I know one guy that lost thirty pounds in "jail" in just fifteen days.

Another time, before I was assigned a job other than picking up cigarette butts, I had fallen asleep in my bunk when I was awakened by my bunkie (the person who slept beside me). He was returning my ID that was also used to access our bank for the purchase of commissary items. They said that when I had laid down, someone had stolen it and tried to use it. They had heard about it and got it back. I have hundreds of stories that occurred in the course of my twenty months in the Department of Corrections. Why I was worthy to have so many guardian angels, both inmates and DoC employees, both civilian and officers, as well as many others outside the system, is still unknown to me. I am so thankful that with all bad things I saw and heard about, I never again felt like I was in danger, except maybe by the press.

I had a number of meetings with my classification officer. She was very nice, seemed very concerned about my wellbeing, and was one of the most caring people I would run across while in DoC. Hope spoke to her every so often about how I was doing, and she told her I was fine. She said that medical had turned me down for the work camp, and that she could get me to a faith based camp but she recommend a reentry program until work release. She said it would take about six month to get my security level to community. I think she did what she could to get me the job I would wind up with.

One of the hardest things to get used to is how slow everything moves in DoC. I guess this should be expected since it is a very big government agency whose primary responsibility is to store human beings; and the DoC did not pick the inmates in their custody, the courts did. Maybe they were not that slow moving, maybe the business world I had been in for twenty-five years had moved that fast. I think this is an appropriate time to say that regardless of all of my comments in this book about government agencies and bureaucrats and the people that work with them, there are so many hard working, caring people that just want to do the right thing and execute the job they were hired to do. That is especially true of DoC, it is a very big agency whose sole purpose is to keep people locked up or supervised. I had always thought that instead of the Department of Corrections it should be called the department of human storage. I think the majority of the DoC employees do the best they can with what they have to work with, which is very limited. The entire time that I was in DoC, I heard that corruption was rampant and that makes it even harder, with the limited resources, to get things done. If that is true, I never personally witnessed it. I could definitely see the inefficiency everywhere, not corruption per se, but maybe the effects of it. Some of that came from having people in positions of leadership, or in charge, that just were not leaders; some not even competent to be anything above a dorm guard, yet they were in charge. It often seemed their number one job was to prove they were in charge, and whatever their true job assignment was came second. But most did the best they could, and when shown courtesy and respect they returned it. A few were just not nice people and seemed to live to show it. I saw a number of guards who kept pushing people, verbally or psychologically, until they snapped and did something wrong to get put in "jail" or worse, shipped out. The DoC has what is commonly referred to as rogue guards who decide that depending on your crime they will punish you more often with beatings done out of the site of others. I have heard the results of this but never witnessed it outside of the reception center.

I now counsel families on procedures or who to contact if it happens to a loved one they know. If any of the above happens and you hear about it there is nothing you can do. It is not like you dial 911 and someone shows up at the prison to save you, as they are not getting in without permission no matter who they are. But life has something for everyone, and those that are bad will face their day of judgment, and those that are good will get their rewards. It was simply time for me to live, learn, remain humble, and savor my lessons. I did thank God often for the nice ones and the ones that seemed to keep an eye on me: inmates, DoC employees, and folks outside checking on me consistently.

I had not seen or talked to my wife and children since the morning of April 9th when I went off to court for my final hearing. I had not been approved for phone privileges or visitation, and therefore was still communicating by mail. On Saturday morning, May 22, 2010, when the guard in the dorm said Holley you have a visitor, I said that is not possible as I have no one approved. He said it could be one of your attorneys, as they would be on your approved visitors list. It took me what I thought was an eternity to get ready and make my way to the visitation center. All inmates are strip-searched into and out of the visitation center. As you can imagine, it's time consuming. So I have no idea how long it took me to get to the visitation center once I was told I had a visitor. I scanned the room, and at the far end of the room was my wife, Hope, sitting there in all her radiant beauty and unforgettable smile. Words cannot express the joy and shock that came over me. She had completed the paperwork and I had turned it in, but I had not heard anything. She was approved for a visit. She kept calling and had found out before I did that she could visit. She said I turned white, and she thought I was going to faint. I cannot remember what we talked about or what I said, only the sheer joy that I had in her being there. It was the first time I had felt semi-normal since April 9th. The time just flew by that day; and the next day, Sunday, my mom came and we had a great visit talking about everything and everybody. My mom then informed me that Hope and my son Christopher were coming around noon, and I started crying. On the one hand, I did not want Christopher coming into that environment, and on the other hand, I missed him so much and wanted to see him. My mom said he would be fine and that keeping him away would be worse. She was right, and I was so happy to see him. My mom taught me a lesson during all this that we have since discussed in more details. That is, when you try to shelter loved one's from hurtful or bad things it is often worse than the truth, as they already know something is wrong, and what goes on in their mind or what they think is wrong might be worse than reality.

My bunkies taught me about currency behind the wire, as money is not allowed on compound and only in visitation with my family or friends. We cannot have money on us, and as I explained earlier the only legitimate way to buy something was using our bank that we accessed with our ID cards. However a very simple yet clever currency has developed inside the system. Inmates buy "commodities" using their bank at the canteen. Primarily used were coffee, cigarettes (no longer allowed), and soups. Yes, ramen noodle soup, the kind you get at the store for pennies a piece. We paid about fifty cents apiece for them. So "soups" were a fifty cents piece, cigarettes were whatever the market would bare, and I think a bag of coffee was five dollars. This was used to pay other inmates for services such as doing laundry or some other chore. It was also used to gamble or to buy some other item someone had that you did not. You could also buy nicer sheets, prison uniforms, pillows, and in the winter you could buy or rent blankets. I rented an extra blanket in the winter. I still have and use a set of cheater dime-store reading glasses that I keep with me at all times to use, and yes, keep me humble and remind me of my lessons learned. I paid two soups for them.

I had visits every single weekend after that; and the week after Hope's first visit, my phone privileges went live. I am told that less than 5% of the prison population receives visits at a regular interval. At this prison, it was about 4%, except on Father's Day and Mother's Day. I took count every weekend and logged it in my journal. That is just sad because I lived and survived week to week on the hope of my weekend visits. I cannot even comprehend what it was like for my wife to arrange weekend visits, not only for herself but for others, so that I would have visitation every weekend. The DoC limits you to fifteen approved visitors, and that just seems so unfair. What is the difference in tracking fifteen people or fifty people in a computer system. I think that rule was made years ago, and now that technology has the ability to track more people just as easily, they need to update it. The more visitors the better for the inmate, and the better the inmate the more smoothly the institution is going to run.

My wife was also working full time, and was a full-time student in a Master's program at Florida Southern College in Lakeland, Florida while this was going on. My mother, her husband, and my sister also drove about three hours on weekends to visit, while Hope had to drive about four hours each way every weekend. It is so sad that so many families simply can't spend the money or have the desire to make the visits. I am told that 75% of prison beds in Florida are North and East of the I-4 corridor in Central Florida, while 75% of the prisoners come from the I-4 corridor and South, meaning most have a ways to drive. For some, it is just cost prohibitive to make the long drives in Florida, which probably contributes to the low visitation rate. Once again, I think that DoC could do a better job keeping those with approved visitors close to home, as I think that visits with family are a positive part of reentering society from these facilities, and those inmates with intact families should be kept closer to them. But all are treated the same, regardless.

I settled in and time began to pass as I read, wrote letters, and kept communication with classification about a job other than "wellness." I also lobbied my dorm sergeant and the sergeant over at visitation (viso) to help me get a job where I volunteered to clean up after "viso." The officers at "viso" were almost always the same, and I really liked them; they were nice. Visitation is DoC's primary contact with the public. So I think, big emphasis on think, they try to put their best foot forward, and most guards, not all, that work it always seemed to be nicer.

I was now receiving a lot of mail, sometime a dozen letters a day, which was such great comfort. I still have them all in a box and plan to read them all again sometime, maybe in preparation for a sequel to this book. One of the letters was from a longtime friend, "Doc" Dockery. He had been friends with my mentor, Tommy Thomas, and as a result of that I met him when I first moved to Lakeland. We then served on several boards and worked political campaigns together. His wife was currently a Florida Senator. She too had become a good friend, and I had worked on a number of her political campaigns. Doc stated in his letter that they were coming to visit me. No date or explanation was given, so I just assumed they would get a special visit similar to an attorney.

As time moved on, and I waited for what was next and for a job, it got hot in a hurry. There are so many notes in my journal about how hot it was. Most just say today was "hot, hot, and hot." The guards were telling me it was getting to the upper 90s, and it was at least that hot in the dorm. We just sweated all the time. The water cooler in the dorm did not work, so we had to drink water out of the sinks and showers, which was warmer than room temperature.

The job posting came out and I had a job as an orderly in the cabinet shop. Wow, I had a job, which was great. Several of my "bunkies" said that meant I would be moving to the H dorm on the other side of the compound. I had become comfortable and did not want to move, but I wanted a job. Most in the dorm I was in did not have jobs except for rec yard, houseman, or wellness; not sure why.

While I was in the infirmary waiting room to see medical, the orderly came and got me and told me to see the officer inside. I saw the officer who I had spoken to about the medical orderly job, and he pointed to the guard in the "bubble." I went in, and he told me to sit down while he looked up something. Then he showed me an article about my transfer to Hamilton that had been put on the DoC website. He asked, "Did you know you are famous?" I said more like infamous and laughed. He was one of the tougher guards on the compound, but I didn't have much interaction with him. He then asked me if I knew what all the commotion on the compound was about. I said, "What commotion?" He replied "You know, the cleaning, painting, and repairs that were going on." I truly had not noticed. By now, several guards were standing in the bubble with us, and one of them asked "Do you know a sitting Senator?" Nervous and not knowing what to say, I said, "I know several." They asked if one was a female Senator. I said yes. They said, "Well there is a high profile visitor coming to the camp to see you…It is a female Senator." I finished medical and was sent back to my dorm. Keeping in mind that all I knew was what was told to me by the guards, and that was not much, I was pretty nervous. Word was getting around someone big was coming to the camp, and a few people knew they were coming to see me.

Then on June 17th, I had a number of call outs, legal mail, a report to my new job, and a call out to classification. One officer said the word was getting out, so you might want to lie to those that were asking what was going on. They said, "Just tell them you have a legal visit." The legal mail call out was a letter from Sen. Paula

Dockery's office stating that she and her husband, Doc, would be in to see me and the date that was given was that day. Wow, nothing like timely mail. That day would be my strangest and busiest since my arrival in DoC custody. The day was made even stranger and more stressful because of the big to do the camp made of it. After legal mail, I tried to go to work, which was on the other side of the camp. I spoke to the guard at the crossing, and he said I was not supposed to cross without a pass, but it did not matter because the cabinet shop was closed that day, and I should return to my dorm.

When I got to the dorm, they were calling for mandatory recreation. I wanted to be at work, but before I could leave for the rec yard one of the Sergeants came in and asked to see me in the bubble. She said she would be with me for the visit and to get showered and put on my best uniform. Then she said she would be back for me in a little while. By now, inmates were asking a lot of questions about what was going on and what the weird call out was for. This visit caused me a number of issues before it happened, to the point that one guard suggested I lie to inmates that heard about it. This visit made many at the camp suspicious of me, both inmates and guards.

The Major of the prison came to the dorm along with the Sergeant that had come earlier. I had never seen him in our dorm in my almost two months there. I was washing up in the bathroom, visible from the bubble, and someone said the Major wanted to see me inside the bubble in the dorm. Every eye in the dorm was on me. As I walked from the bathroom to the bubble, maybe twenty feet, I thought, "Oh, this is not good." The Major then asked if I was ok, and were those my best clothes and shoes. I said I was fine and these were my best clothes. They were rags, and all I had for shoes was what we called bobos, or cheap slip on tennis shoes. He told the dorm officer to call laundry and get me a new uniform and new boots. The officer asked my sizes and I gave them to him. The Major then looked at me again and asked, "Is everything alright?" I replied, "Yes, I am fine, and I am sorry about all the commotion." He said "Its fine, get showered, a haircut, and go pick up your clothes." Then he left the dorm. Every eye in the dorm was still on me as the Major left. The Sergeant then took me to laundry to get my new clothes; the Sergeant over the laundry did not look happy. We then headed back to the dorm for me to get ready. Walking back to the dorm, we passed the Sergeant from visitation that I always volunteered to help. She said with a smile, "So my helper is the famous one." The Sergeant walking with me replied, "Yes he is." She then said, "Well, he is a good worker." I replied, "I will see you this weekend."

Back at the dorm, all eyes were on me, and the inmates were asking me what was going on. After I showered and got dressed, the Sergeant came back, and once count cleared she took me to early chow. I told her there is no way I could eat. So we went to the classification/medical building to wait. My classification officer came out and said I would like my new job and the teacher there. She also said they should have just taken me to the administration building, which was on the same property but outside the prison compound, for my visit and then the Senator could take her tour and no one would have known the difference. That made way too much sense, so no way was it going to happen that way.

I heard them call on the radio that the Senator was in the parking lot. They cleared medical and classification of inmates, and I was taken to a room that I had never been in. Sort of a sparsely furnished conference room. I sat there until Doc and Paul came in, and we visited for about an hour. We talked about everyone and everything we could in that time, and I felt normal for that hour or so. They then said they had to take the tour of the prison, and they exited the same way they came in. I was so appreciative of them taking the time and coming so far out of their way to visit me. It truly meant so much. Even with all the commotion and unnecessary drama, I was very glad they had come to visit me. I have never ask her what she saw in her tour or what they let her see.

They should have let me give her the tour. That would have been a big laugh. Afterward, I waited in medical/classification with the officer in the bubble until the tour was over and she had exited the compound; it was air conditioned and the dorm was probably a 100 degrees. I did not see her or Doc again, as they had the compound locked down.

They sent me back to my dorm about 3:15 p.m. The Sergeant that had been with me in the morning returned to the dorm. She said that quite a commotion had been made of this and that if I felt threatened or scared to let someone know, and that there was a chance I would be transferred for my safety. The dorm officer said basically the same thing. I had told most that I had a high profile lawyer visit, and many did not connect the two visits as being the same. However, many did, and everyone was asking what had gone on and where I had been during the lockdown. Big John told me he was just happy to have an important friend no matter what was going on. After shift change, and while we were heading out to chow, the night officer told me to stay back for a minute. He said he was a little worried and to let him know if I had any problems during the night. He also said he thought I would be transferred within days. The day ended with a lousy meal and a couple of really long "counts." It was a hot and loud night and the Lakers beat Boston in game 7 in L.A. I spoke to Hope several times that night and brought her up to speed on what had happened. I had a hard time going to sleep, so I wrote Doc and Paula a thank you card and lay in my bunk just sweating beads. A long exciting day had come to a close.

The next day I had a medical call out, probably to make sure I was alive. I was fine, and everyone in the dorm was just curious; no problems at all. Medical was for a blood pressure check and it was 133/93, not bad considering the stress of the prior day. They then told me I had daily blood pressure checks for three days. They were going to keep me alive now, for sure. Actually, I heard later that the blood pressure checks were to get me sent to the work camp, but medical would not sign off on it.

My mom and her husband visited that weekend, and by the time I got into "viso" the Sergeant and the guards had brought her and Wayne up to speed on my week. They told her I would probably be transferred out in the coming days. It was a busy day at visitation with over fifty inmates there. I hated it being crowded but was glad to see more inmates getting visits. Still only 4.5% of camp got visitors that day, and that was a big day. I was moved to H dorm that weekend, as everyone said I would be getting the new job.

I did finally start my regular job on Monday. Everyone in this dorm worked or went to school, so it was a different atmosphere. I would be working in the cabinet shop that built cabinets for other institutions. The instructor was a civilian and over the cabinet shop, as it was both a production facility and a teaching facility. I was deemed to be an orderly, that means cleanup person, but I did whatever I was asked including helping to build cabinets. The instructor was quite good at what he did. There was also a brick mason shop next door to us and an electrical shop next to it. Between the cabinet shop and the mason shop, I have to say how shocked I was at the talented people that worked and graduated from these programs. It's a shame that there is no funding to give anyone who wishes to complete these courses the opportunity. That would truly be rehabilitation (corrections) and would, in fact, give people some working skills; and as I said, all three instructors were very good, at least from what I observed in my interactions with them. This was a much better job than picking up cigarette butts, and the time passed so much faster when working that I wish we could have worked eighty hours a week. It sure beat being locked in the dorm. It was very hot in the shop in the summer, but it had fans and a very cold water fountain; two luxuries I would never again take for granted. The dorm was even hotter with no fans, well they did have exhaust fans when they worked. Even though I was just an orderly, the instructor and my boss took the time to answer my questions and teach me how to build cabinets when he was able. This was a place where time finally started to move.

The following weeks were busy with work, visitations, and a number of medical call outs: chest X Ray, EKG, blood work, and of course blood pressure checks. Yes sir, they were going to keep me alive now; of course this camp did not know about the blood pressure debacle at the reception center. Hope and the kids had taken a little vacation so mom and Wayne came up both days for two weekends. My sister, Sally, got approved and came with them. Then a couple more friends got approved, and before long I was at my maximum approval of fifteen visitors. I hoped this would take some pressure off Hope, but other than during that vacation she still came every weekend, as did my mom and Wayne. Wow, what a sacrifice.

Over the next couple of weeks, we built a bunch of book cases. Early on, we had to cut them down for a change order and then build a bunch more of the new size. As I said, we were busy and the time passed by so fast.

There are about three weeks that I have no entry in my journal. That is probably a result of being busy and with working, visitations, and spending my spare time answering letters. During this time, I was cut by some kind of object in a garbage bag while volunteering at visitation. They took me to medical; I weighed in at 216 ½ pounds and my blood pressure was 122/72. Wow, had I come a long way in a few months. In August, Trey and Carter were approved to visit, and I got to see them. One of my first entries in my journal after the long absence was about the heat. The dorm officer and I guessed it was over a 100 degrees in the dorm. Not sure what kind of sauna type environment it takes to lie in bed and sweat, but we did every night until one or two in the morning. Try to sleep with beads of sweet rolling down your back; it's like some kind of torture. I would have taken weekly water boarding in exchange for a big fan or an air conditioning unit.

While in this dorm, I began to speak with a lot of people. Some of the guys would use religion or conversations about religion as a con to try and get something out of you. Once, I was having a conversation with a young man about religion. He gave me my first nickname: Dr. Phil. I had seen and heard how he was acting on the basketball court, using the language and the actions that were not the same as he was speaking to me. During one of our conversations I said, "Don't tell me about your religion or faith, show me." He looked at me funny and asked, "What do you mean?" I said, "You know, when you're out there talking to your 'home boys' playing basketball or playing cards, show me your religion." I think, at first he thought that I was trying to be funny, or even worse that I was messing with him. In a couple of days he came back and spoke to me again. I told him that I knew he had a good heart, and I did, in fact, believe that he believed in something bigger than himself. I went on to say that the practicing of your faith was to be done all the time not just when it was convenient or in church. I could tell that this was a special young man with a big heart. I realized then that these young men were not evil people. Many that I met had big hearts but were made out to be very evil. Unfortunately they did not have so great of an upbringing and had made some real bad choices. The majority of them had never been told they did a good job at something, or maybe even heard the words, "I love you." So many had been given bad advice, both legal and personal, either by peers or even legal counsel. I believe with all my heart that God reawakened my ability to interact with all walks of people and to see their hearts and read their feelings, much as I had done while working on the fishing boats or selling cars. I used that gift to speak to as many as I could in the short period of time that I was there. I interacted with them, having no idea what kind of impact I might have been making. It was truly better therapy for me, but I enjoyed the interaction with so many from all walks of life. Sometimes, I would just help someone read their mail or understand a doctor's order on a prescription, and in some cases I read legal mail and gave them my interpretation on what it said. Since all those of faith believe that we are on a journey, and that on that journey we are given free will and wisdom by God. We also know that on this journey we will take misdirection's and be allowed to suffer the consequences of those actions. The simplest way to see the correct course is with prayer, meditation, and by helping others. In many cases, helping others is not about writing a check but about volunteering time to help them with situations they believe to be out of their grasp, or just by showing that you care about them.

All inmates in prison have nicknames; I had several. As I said, the first was "Dr. Phil," the others were "The Senator," "Old School," and "Pops." The last two are generic to any inmate older than the average. I was only forty-nine years old, but yes I was Old School or Pops to these guys. Many just called me Mr. Holley, something I had rarely been called because I always thought that Mr. Holley was my dad. Kind of funny, but I would sometimes refer to my dad as "Pops" and my son will sometimes call me Pops.

I volunteered to stay after visitation on Saturdays and Sundays to help clean up. At the main unit at Hamilton there were a couple of corrections officers, both female, one a Sergeant and the other officer. They genuinely seem to appreciate my efforts to make the grounds look as good as possible. For some reason, the administration had decided that visitation no longer needed orderlies on weekends. That was fine with me, as I enjoyed the extra hour a day of not being in the dorm, particularly in the summer when the dorm could reach a 100 degrees. It also gave me a chance to interact with a couple of the other volunteers that were not from my dorm. There is something about cleaning up an area for no other reason than it feels good to do it.

August 10, 2010 had already started out to be a weird day. Our side of the compound had been locked down, so they could shake down (more on that term later when it happened to me) G dorm. It was late morning before we got to work, and it was also a mass (church service) for me; so I went. I returned to the cabinet shop to work, and we were wrapping up the day pretty much as usual, not having gotten much done that day. All tools at the cabinet shop are checked in and checked out every day, as you can well imagine they do not want hammers and nail guns, along with a lot of other tools, unaccounted for in a prison environment. At 3:40 p.m. it was discovered that a special tool from the paint shop (we had a paint booth to paint cabinets) was missing from inventory. So we all started looking for it, and the inmates that had started to leave were recalled to also help look. The officer over the school/shop area, a very good and conscientious corrections officer, arrived, gathered everyone, and said we need to find the tool. This tool was a wrench, and its only purpose was to take apart the mask used in the paint shop. It had no value to anyone other than possibly a weapon. I guess you could make a weapon out of anything, but there were so many other items that could have been used that we were all sure that it had been misplaced or lost, not stolen. About 4:00 p.m. other guards showed up, and shortly after that the Captain of day shift came in. He was, in my opinion, the best white shirt, Lieutenant, Captain, or Major, at Hamilton that I had met. By 4:15, there were a dozen or so officers in the shop, all yelling and screaming about finding the tool. We were then all stripped naked and searched. The Captain I had referenced left, and the Major, mentioned earlier in the book, and the night-time Captain arrived. This was getting way out of hand. Then the evening-shift Captain said, "If we do not find this tool everyone goes to jail." He said it right in from of the Major and all the other guards. Now I have seen some bureaucrats of rank back themselves in to a corner before, but wow, this one took the cake. One of the officers standing behind me said to another officer that there was not that much room in confinement. So here I am standing in my boxers, they let us put them on, thinking here goes work release; I'm going to miss my phone call to Hope tonight; and I am going to be locked up for something I had nothing to do with, no control over, and would not know what the tool was if I saw it. Then visions of being in the box in August, missing visitation, losing another fifty pounds I no longer had to lose, and all kinds of other horrors stories starting

coming into my mind. I thought I was going to throw up. I had butterflies in my stomach the size of bats.

Then the instructor, probably the most level headed guy in the
room at the time, said that he did not believe that it was missing. So
he, the tool man in charge of inventorying tools, the inmate that
lost it, and the Major all go back in the tool room that might be 10
x 20 feet and full of tools. I thought to myself if they find that tool
I am going to scream. You guessed it, they found the tool mixed
in with a pile of extension cords in the tool room. Now, if you can
just picture this keystone-cop episode unfolding before your very
eyes. You would have thought that everyone was just happy it was
over. Nope, not in DoC, the Major ordered the tool man and the
painter that had checked out the tool to be locked up in confinement, "jail", and the Major left.

As we were getting dressed and ready to line up and head back
to our dorms, the big discussion between the instructor and the
white shirts in the room was who was going to write the DR and
what were they going to write it for: A tool that was just inches away
from where it should be in the tool room and was missing but was
not missing? I do not know the outcome, but I heard that they issued a cc or incident report and the two guys were to be let out in
a day or two. They were back at work within a few days, as mad as
they could be about losing their bunks and all the stuff they were
put through.

On August 13th, I was sent to medical for chest x-rays, blood
pressure check, and an EKG. Weight fully dressed was 207 ½
pounds, blood pressure was 112/77, temperature was normal. All
the bloodwork that had been done in the past, and I never was told
results. All was perfect, so the doctor said.

A week or so later, an inmate from Parry Florida, Country was
his nick name, and I were talking, and he said to me, "We should
call an animal right's organization and tell them that they have
seventy-two purebred German Shepherds locked up in a 120 by 40
foot block building with no climate control and warm water. They

are punished if they use the bathroom without permission, and given 90 degree water on 100 degree days. List the food fed daily, mainly bean and soy bean based meals. They would go nuts until they found out it was inmates instead of animals."

"Be at war with your vices, at peace with your neighbors, and let every New Year find you a better man."

— Benjamin Franklin

14

DAYS, WEEKS, AND MONTHS PASS THROUGH THE SYSTEM

On September 13, 2010, I was transferred to the work camp a few hundred yards from the main unit. This is a good time to say that as I was leaving the main unit of Hamilton CI after some four months here, many people approached me to see what was going on, and many I had spent so much time with said their goodbyes. With all the stories I tell in this book about how bad so much of this was, there were so many good hearted inmates and corrections officers, and so many of them had been my guardian angels at some point or many points in the last four months. I have reached out to a few since then, but not many. So many of the inmates just want to do their time, and so many of the officers truly do try to make a difference to those that seek to be better. I regret not being able to list all the names of all those that helped me get through this part of my life's journey.

The work camp was a much smaller facility with about 200 inmates. This also meant I lost my job at the cabinet shop. The work camp supplied work and maintenance crews to a number of state and city agencies, as well as the prison compound itself. My security level was changed to Community Control the week that I was moved. That was the level needed to be in work release; it also allowed you to work outside of the gate with little or no supervision. However, I was never allowed to go out the gate. I worked in the kitchen for a few weeks and then as a "houseman" janitor in the dorm. We always suspected that my elevated visibility was the reason, however, that is a guess on my part because I was never told why I could not go out the gate. The rumor mill, we referred to that as "inmate.com," of the older inmates that worked in the administration building and some of the other offices was that there were things going on that they did not want me to see, but that was just rumor. I was the only community control inmate that did not go out the gate on a daily basis, and that was a fact.

It was also during this time that I was taken to medical for a work release physical. It was at the annex complex where I had originally arrived at Hamilton CI. The doctor, who I could barely understand due to his broken English and accent, asked me if I had brought my fingers and toes. I said yes, thinking he was kidding. He then said, "Show me." You had to laugh at hearing that with his accent. He asked if I had been raped, and I said no. He then asked if I thought I had any sexually transmitted diseases; I said no. Then he said that after getting out I should remember to practice safe sex. I told him I was happily married and planned to remain monogamous. Well, he said, just the same it was his job to tell me and that I had passed the work release physical. I said, "Good, can I go now?" He jumped to his feet and said, "NO, you must wait until approved to go to work release." I told him I meant back to the waiting room to sit with the others. He then sheepishly said, "Yes you can." Did he not realize I was in a prison and could not walk out even if I wanted to? You cannot make this stuff up.

We then made the half mile or so drive back from the annex to the work camp. They opened the gate but forgot to take down a steel cable used to keep vehicles from running the gate. We rolled into the cable and it broke the grill of the van. We waited around for about thirty minutes in the hot sun for someone to make a decision as to what to do. They sent us back to medical for a check up to make sure we were all alright. Not sure what happened to the rest, but a nurse sat me down and asked if I was hurt. I said, "I don't think so. But could I call my lawyer and check?" She was not amused. I thought it was hilarious, but her, not so much!

Visitation at this camp was very small with very few people. It was much more comfortable and relaxed, and that of course meant a lot. The sergeant of our dorm at night was a lady that had been at the camp a very long time and ran a very tight ship. She was always very nice to me, very fair to all that did what they were supposed to do, and tough on the ones that did not.

On September 16th, I was working on the grounds doing a project for one of the sergeants and was approached by two sergeants. They asked if I knew what was going on. Of course I had no way of knowing anything, but I guess they assumed I did. They said I was getting a high profile visit, and they did not know who it was. About this time, I was paged to the lieutenant's "LT" office. The lieutenant said I had a visit, and that I was to go get a haircut, shower, and put on my visitation blues. I was to stay in the dorm and wait until someone came and got me. I thought, here we go again.

About 1:45 p.m. I was told by the dorm officer to go to the lieutenant's office for further instructions. I was again asked if those were my best clothes, and I told the "LT" that they were. He said to go sit in the visitation park. A couple of the sergeants and officers would pass through to check on me; I think most were just curious as to who was coming. One asked if it was the Senator again, as that was the rumor. I said I truly did not know what was going on or who was coming, as I had not received any letters and my wife had not mentioned it. About 4:00 p.m. no one had arrived, and I was told to return to my dorm for count.

A few weeks later, I was again told to prepare for a special visit and not too much was made of it this time. It was a longtime friend, State Representative Seth McKeel and his wife Kim. We had been friends since before they were married, and I was so happy to see them. We talked kids, family, and of course a little politics. The warden stopped by to say hello to Seth and did not look at or speak to me. It was the first and only time that I would see him in my time at Hamilton CI. I was so appreciative of Seth and Kim for stopping by. Seth's father, another longtime friend, was very ill and he and Seth were very close. So the extra time away from home to visit was so special, and I felt so guilty that I could not be with them during this difficult time. His father would pass away before I would return to freedom, and it hurt that I could not be with Seth and his wonderful family during this time. Seth and Kim remain close friends of Hope and mine.

I have to tell one more prison story before moving on from here. I was assigned to the kitchen for a short period of time. I was the only community control inmate working the kitchen, but that is not the point of the story. Like with the cabinet shop, we checked out tools and utensils for cooking and serving meals. At the end of one of the days, a serving scope was missing and it was checked out in my name. I was the head of the line and served the main course, whatever that was, and this was a small scoop used for serving butter or ketchup. The officer said, "Well, it is checked out in your name, so you will be the one to go to "jail" if it is not found." I was highly ticked off; he had checked it out, and he had written down the wrong name, and now it was my problem. As usual, the sergeant and lieutenant came in, and this was again getting out of hand. Finally, the civilian that was in charge of the food and cooking took control and said, let's find this thing. It was in a vat of ketchup in the cooler at the bottom of course. I do not know how she found it. She told the guard that whoever served the ketchup should go to "jail" since they probably put it there on purpose so as not to have to wash it. Nothing else happened; we finished cleaning, and they sent us to our dorms. Another hour of butterflies and yelling and screaming for nothing. Shortly after this, I was moved to houseman and would spend my remaining time at the work camp cleaning.

PINSTRIPE SUITS TO PRISON BLUES

On October 10, 2010, my friend Dennis Hood and his long-time girlfriend Mary Jo were married; they had planned for about a year to be married on 10/10/10. There are so many things that you miss when you lose your freedom, some you take with a grain of salt, and others weigh on you heavily. This really bothered me to not be there with my friend, as well as dozens of other events for my family.

On or about October 13, 2010, I was told late in the day to pack my things and report to the LT's office. I asked the dorm guard what was going on and where was I going. He said he had no idea, but to hurry. Everyone in the dorm was asking what was going on, and I said I had no idea. After reporting to the LT's office, I again asked what was going on. He said, "Don't you know what is going on?" I said I had no idea. He said, "Well, I don't believe you. If you don't know, I cannot tell you, but I am sure someone will." I sat in visitation for a little while; I felt like I was going to throw up I was so nervous. All the work crews were returning to the camp. I sat there through chow and then count, and then was loaded in a van and taken to Lake Butler for the night. It was a long stressful night, but I have told enough stories about stress and being scared.

The next day I was transferred to the Orlando Reception Center where I had departed some six months earlier. I sat there for a week, but got to visit with Hope and my mom in the biggest and emptiest visitation center I had been in. I was able to speak again to the dorm sergeant I liked. I spent a fairly uneventful week, having no interaction with the guards that had assaulted me or others during my last visit, although I saw them both. At 3 a.m. the door rolled open, and they called my name to pack.

"To succeed in life, you need two things:
ignorance and confidence."

— Mark Twain

15

NEW SOULS TO LEARN FROM

O n October 20, 2010, I arrived at Polk Correctional in Polk City FL, just thirty miles from home. Polk CI was transitioning into a reentry camp for inmates with less than three years remaining in their sentence who would be released in Hillsborough or Polk County Florida. It has long been considered by inmates and guards alike to be one of the better camps in the Florida DoC systems.

During the previous week's ordeal and transfers, I thought I was on my way to work release. Several people told me I was on my way to a better place, but no specifics, so I just assumed work release. But that was not yet to be. I had applied for work release at Hamilton, but something had happened to some of the paperwork. I had to complete the process at Polk, and they said they did not think it would cost me any time or delay getting to work release, but one never knows. We were again shackled for the transfer. Even though I was community control some of the others were not.

Upon arrival I was checked over by a nurse and my blood pressure was 122/82, which is very good for me, but the big surprise was my weight was now 197 ½ pounds, the lowest it had been in thirty years. Many of the guards at this camp knew me; I was now back in my own backyard. Unlike some of the other camps, almost everyone I would encounter at this prison was nice: guards, civilians, administration, and inmates for the most part.

On Friday, after having been at this new camp for two days, I would go before a panel of officers. I believe the camp colonel sat on this panel, and the classification staff for job assignment. I do not think that Hamilton had a colonel, if so I never saw him or her. This seemed to be an open forum, and from my short exposure to this process they seemed to be trying to place the inmate in the best job for himself and the institution. This was dramatically different from job placement procedures at Hamilton.

It was widely discussed that I should be in the automotive vocational building to help teach, which sounded good to me. However, it was then discovered that I was already community control and had to go to the work camp to "exercise my custody level." I thought, wow here we go again to the work camp just to sit there, because if DoC would not let me go out the gate in Hamilton County there's no way they're going to let me out in my own back yard. It was decided that I would go to the work camp that afternoon. I thanked the panel and went back to my dorm, nothing to do but wait on visitation and visit with the inmates in my dorm. Several of the "old timers" were still in this dorm awaiting the inevitable transfer to a camp for inmates with long sentence. Several of these men had life sentences but knew of me. They were very nice, and I chatted with a number of them for hours. One that is now deceased was the landlord of one of my long time employees, so he felt like he knew me.

I spent almost seven days on the main compound before being transferred. Polk CI was still transitioning into a reentry camp, so many of the lifers and others with long sentences were still on the compound a lot of them were very old and had numerous health issues. Many had the same bunk and dorm for years and were very upset about having to be transferred. They desired to pass their remaining time in peace, as much of that as you can have in prison anyway.

I came to realize that so many of these men that were convicted of horrible crimes were simply not the same people they had been when they were tried and convicted. Some were people who just seemed like someone's grandfather, in fact, many of them were. I understand their crimes had changed lives, but I think this is a good time to remember that when you have a person convicted of a crime and sent away for a long time, two families are changed forever: the victim's and the family of the accused or convicted. Months later, I would hear that many of the inmates did not transition well to the other prisons and were having very difficult times; many died in a fairly short time frame. As I said, many were in bad health already, so I am sure the stress of the move did not help. Some of them may have been ready to die, although none expressed that to me. Keep in mind that due to their age it is predetermined that most of these men will die in prison for the crimes they committed, even if that was not their sentence.

I cannot say when the appropriate time is to insert this, but over the past years I have seen government agencies get things so wrong that it is very hard for me to support anything that is so absolute as the death penalty. I do not want that to be the focus of this book, and it is more of a personal view now not a political one. But they can and do get it wrong, and even if that is just one time then that is one too many. You frequently hear in the news of someone who was wrongfully accused or convicted being released as a result of some new evidence, DNA testing, or a witness that recanted on their death bed. You get the picture. I spent many hours talking, and more importantly listening to many of these men. I have so often stated in this book, I feel I have the ability to read people, feel people's hearts, and understand things beyond my educational level. So I can say with great conviction that many of these men are not who they were or who they are portrayed to be. I know that with all my heart most of these people are not evil, but at one time they did evil things and made very bad decisions, many of them as a result of drug or alcohol use or abuse, even though that might not have been one of the charges. I understand that is not a defense for bad actions, but when clean they are different people. I was a staunch conservative in my political views for most of my life, but I have changed some of my thoughts and views toward the convicted or accused, and for many other lost souls, as well. The majority of Americans are religious people that believe in God and truly want to help others in this world, but it is just so easy, and sometimes even politically correct, to write off a convicted man or women as evil.

We often substitute what could be for what is enthusiastically portrayed as factual in the media. I can tell you the true facts of a case are rarely completely accurate, and the more high profile the case or story and the more clamoring for information, the less accurate the reporting. Facts do not sell newspapers or improve ratings, but sensationalism does. We now have a saying that media outlets often "do not let the facts get in the way of a good story." It's sort of like the fishing stories the old men around the dock where I grew up used to tell. Sure, they all started out as factual, but then a good storyteller has to juice it up a little over time. I do not believe that most reporters or journalists report incorrect information on purpose, but with so much to report and deadlines to meet, it is just not possible to check everything, and with almost no repercussions for getting it wrong, they don't.

I was not transferred to the work camp on Monday as expected, so I settled in for another night in the main unit. During early evening count, the dorm officer told me to report to the chaplain's office after count clears. Everyone around me said that meant someone had died, as that was the only time you get called to the chaplain's office. Well I had been in long enough so as not to believe everything I heard from "inmate.com," but still in the back of my mind I was worrying about what this could be. This is when I met Chaplain Al Khatib, the Senior chaplain at Polk CI. He was friends with Monsignor Caulfield and had heard I was at Polk, and he wanted to check on me. He is a kind and caring man charged with a monumental task. As a chaplain at a prison, he takes his job to heart with numerous responsibilities, many of them not pleasant. Our paths would cross many times while I was at Polk and since then.

The following day, I was transferred to the work camp. I thought, here we go. After a review with an officer, I was told I would be assigned to a DoT crew. I thought, wow no way they are going to give me a gate pass to be out in the public. So I asked her about it, and she said she had my gate pass in her hand. I thought that was strange since it had been rumored for several days that I would be in the administration building or the warehouse. I had a series of call outs, some of them back at the main unit. I thought, we could have done this while I was sitting around being bored, but I just kept my mouth shut and settled into my new environment. After several days of getting through the call outs, I finally went to work. It was hard work, but it was nice to be out and about in the "real" world. Then a press story hit again about what I was doing, and I was kept in until they sorted it out. I then had another visit from Senator Dockery, with much less fan fair this time. They took me back to the main unit and we met in a classification office. It was nice to see Paula again and catch up. It was also nice that they did not make such a spectacle of it and just let us visit.

After a few days, I was assigned to the warehouse. Although this was still on the prison grounds, it was outside the prison and work camp gates. I would not be out in the real world, but with the press still being relentless on covering my every move this was probably for the best. At the warehouse, we processed supply orders for the main unit and cleaned. My boss there was tough but very fair. She just wanted you to work, obey the rules, and not cause any grief; seemed fair to me. We used to say that we had the cleanest warehouse of any in the state. We mopped it every day, and it was always spotless. Some inmates before us had been caught breaking some rules, and everyone working there was sent to "jail" until it was sorted out. Of course, it was just one or two, but the others had to suffer through the investigation until cleared.

One of the inmates, Louis Resciniti, was a member of my church, but we did not know each other prior to working in the warehouse together. It was about a week, I think, before he was cleared of being involved with whatever happened and returned to the work camp and the warehouse. We worked together and were housed on the same compound, work camp, but in different dorms. He is a man of great faith, and was a pleasure to have worked with. His spiritual guidance while we were together was very enlightening. He also received visits every weekend, so we saw each other's families at visitation.

While here, the time was passing. I would endure a Thanksgiving and Christmas while here, as well as watch as my fiftieth birthday pass. I could have imagined over the years many things I might have been doing for my fiftieth birthday, but this was not one of them.

I made friends with another inmate who worked the canteen (concession stand) in the Visitation Park on weekends, and then worked at the warehouse that resupplied the canteens housed in the same building we worked in. He had been in a long time but was getting near the end of his sentence. His name was Floyd, and we still keep in touch.

At the warehouse, we also had the mail room and prepared supplies for other facilities and other buildings on the compound, including the training building and the administration building that housed the warden and others in the administration offices of the prison. Chaplain would stop by the warehouse and chat with my boss, so I was able to get to know him better. We have kept in touch and had conversation about reentry programs that we share a passion for. He also worked with Father Caulfield and our parish on Catholic Mass's for the Catholic prison population. It is my hope and prayer to teach inside the prison system in some of the faith-based programs. I would like to teach about how to reenter society, which includes opening checking accounts, applying for jobs, apply for credit to get a car or a house. I believe that everyone with the right attitude and aptitude should and can get a second chance.

Time did move faster here, and since most on this compound were short timers, having less than three years remaining, it seemed to be a little or maybe even a lot better. There were much less inmate problems, and the guards really did not seem to provoke much here, except for the one or two rogue officers that seemed to stir the pot.

At this camp, I did witness something that I had heard about in Hamilton but never witnessed, other than the missing tool in the cabinet shop, and that is what was called a "shakedown." I believe in my short time here I would witness three of them. They were supposedly conducted by the Inspector General of the Department of Corrections office. I am not sure if that is true, as the people doing the shakedown seemed like regular guards to us, although I had never seen any of them before. The way this worked was that in the middle of the night they turned on all the lights and start screaming at us to not move, while kicking garbage cans and tipping over stuff. A lot of yelling and screaming seemed to be the prerequisite for all the shakedowns that I witnessed at this camp. We would then be ordered to not touch anything and remain at attention next to our bunks. We would be permitted to put on limited clothes and then escorted out of the dorm to another building like the Visitation Park or library. Someone would go with us and strip us down and search us while they took drug dogs through the dorms and search everything. The first time I witnessed this they trashed the dorm: tipping over garbage cans, flipping over mattresses, and generally making a huge mess of the place. This took several hours, not to mention the fact that they got to go home to bed while we still had to clean up the mess and then get up and go to work. In my time at Polk CI work camp, I was in two different dorms. Both dorms were "shaken down" while I was there, then in the afternoon while we were returning from work. We, all crews that go off the compound, were strip searched everyday on our return to the compound. But on this day it was the guys from the IG, or whoever they were or wherever they came from. They did an extra special strip search and had the dogs smell us and our clothes. To my knowledge, they never found anything, as no one ever went to "jail," so they must not have. When I returned to the dorm after the search I asked the guard on duty, a female, if she had that 800 rape hot-line number. With a surprised look on her face, she asked, "Why?" I said because I had been violated. She just laughed and said, "Find it yourself." Yes, we had female guards in the dorms, open showers and all; and they have male guards at female prisons as well. You would think that would be a recipe for problems, and it sometimes was but none that was reported, that I know of.

I really have not talked about the drugs and the rape situation in prison. I simply never found a good place that it fit. But I will say, I never personally witnessed any sexual abuse, or physical abuse other than what I have already mentioned. Mental abuse was a different story. Some guards really like to mess with people and push their buttons. Many inmates would say or do things to bring it on themselves, but much of the reprisal went above and beyond. I am trying to stick to the facts, so I cannot write about speculation or rumors. There were drugs on every compound I was at: some I heard about, some I smelled, and others I could just tell they were on something. It was the same with cell phones; I heard about their existence but never wanted to know any more than I heard. With all the strip searches and security, I think you can be confident that most of the contraband was not coming from the inmates. I never could figure out why they did not have a drug/contraband dog at every prison or work camp checking every inmate, guard, civilian, sub-contractor, truck, or container coming into the camp. That would have stopped a large percentage of the contraband. But they do not do this, as they would rather wake us up in the middle of the night with the kicking and screaming, or as I used to call it "the dog and pony show."

I truly do wonder how much of it was for show and how many searches were truly intended to find anything or catch anyone. If they truly want to clean some of that stuff up, they should just bring in off duty or retired FBI agents, or police officers that have nothing to do and no association with DoC, and see what they find. My guess is that a lot of folks inside DoC do not want outside eyes inside their prisons. But the drug or contraband dog at the front gate 24/7 would solve a lot of issues, and they already have facilities for taking care of the tracking dogs in case of an escape, so it's a simple and much cheaper solution.

It was during my stay at Polk CI that a group of friends tried to get me clemency to have my sentence reduced, or at least the probation that was hanging over my head and my civil rights restored. This was another very painful leg of this journey. I could write pages about that process. Many thought that I would not get a hearing, but I did, and it was not pretty. People testified that I had done everything possible to ruin lives, and in spite of hundreds of letters in my defense, and my attorney's testimony to all the restitution and restoration of credit, the case was closed almost before it was started, and it caused my wife and my mother much more pain. It also gave the press another field day to cut and paste the stories of the past. But through all this pain, so many friends stepped up to help. There were many professionals working with no pay to help me again. The hundreds of letters that were written saying all the things I had done for people were heartwarming and did keep my faith in spite of the awful outcome. I believe that a number of friends that had worked so hard on the clemency were more hurt and upset than I was. I am so grateful for their efforts, and it truly was the thought that counted, and for that I am a blessed man to have so many friends that have been there for me and my family.

Just before Christmas was very cold and depressing. I had thought I would be on work release by now; and as I faced my first and only Christmas "behind the wire," as well as my fiftieth birthday, I was pretty sad. I slept next to a window, and we had to leave it open slightly to get some air circulation, or those sleeping under the heater would get very hot. My feet froze as the night air came across them, so I rented a blanket from the laundry man. I believe I paid two soups a week for it. The Salvation Army would give us a pair of new socks, a note pad with the Salvation Army shield on it, as well as some candy. You would have thought they gave us a gift card. I was so grateful and proud of an organization that I had given to and supported in the past for doing something so simple and so worthy of God's love. I still have the pair of socks and note pad, and will keep them forever as a reminder of what a great organization can do to help those in need. To the Salvation Army, on behalf of inmates around the world: Thank you!

In late January, it was pretty cold, and we did not seem to be as busy in the warehouse. One day it was rumored that I was being transferred again. I thought, *what, no way*. But the rumors that circulated were that it was to work release. This was the last week of January, and I had now been at Polk CI for just over three months; about the same amount of time since we corrected the paperwork started at Hamilton CI. Sure enough, at 3 a.m. I was awaken by a guard to inventory my property and pack up for the transfer. I had no idea how this worked or where I had to go, but I just assumed I had to go back to the reception center in Orlando; my stomach was in knots again, although I was glad to be getting to work release, something I was originally told would take 90 to 120 days and was now ten months later. Several other transferees were packed up about 6 a.m. to be taken to the main unit to get on the bus to the Orlando Reception Center, but another guy and I were left in the dorm while everyone else went to work. They came and got him and told him a van was picking him up. I just sat around watching the clock tick as my stomach felt like I had bats in it again. Then about 9 a.m. they told me to report to the front gate.

I was taken in a patrol car (no shackles; I even rode in the front seat) to Demilly, a faith based reentry camp that was about a half mile away. It is now closed and vacant as a result of budget cuts. I waited in the guard shack at the main gate until the officer and some other inmates came in from Bartow Work Release. I went in with them, then we went to medical to get checked out and then in the van on our way to Bartow Florida. Now I really was in my backyard. Bartow Florida is the county seat of Polk County and is the town that one of my dealerships had been in. It was about fifteen miles from my house. Driving the streets of Polk County, I was actually feeling pretty normal. The officer was very nice and turned out to be one of my favorites at the camp.

"If you don't read the newspaper, you're uninformed. If you read the newspaper, you're mis-informed."

— Mark Twain

16

A SECOND CHANCE AT ENLIGHTENMENT

I arrived at the Bartow Work Release Center, in Bartow Florida, on January 25, 2011. I was finally at work release with just under eleven months to go in my sentence. As it turned out, this was the least stressful transfer I had experienced in the DoC system: no shackles, and every guard I encountered in Work Release was much more laid back for the most part. This was a much different environment than I had been in since April 9, 2010. It looked more like a weekend camp than something run by the Department of Corrections. It didn't even have much of a fence and no gate, but all the personnel were DoC people and wore the same uniforms as those behind the wire. (Being behind the wire is what inmates and guards call being in the real prison environment.) We did not have to wear prison uniforms. In fact, I was loaned a pair of jeans and a shirt within hours of arriving and never put on a prison uniform again except to go back to Demilly or Polk CI to medical.

The first day was pretty uneventful, as we were given an orientation and told the rules of the camp. They asked who had a driver's license and social security card since we would need them to work, even though we were not allowed to drive. We were then assigned to a dorm for those that were new or did not work. It was a four-man dorm, and that was a lot more private than anything I had seen for a long time.

The food was better there, and we were allowed to have a family member bring us work clothes and a few other things we would need, as there was no canteen or commissary on this compound. After we started working, or had money in our accounts, we went to Walmart, Dollar Tree, or Dollar General every few weeks to pick up what we needed as far as incidentals.

I was encouraged by a sergeant at the work camp to attend a class called Second Chance. This was a class based on the three principle teachings of Sydney Banks. My first meeting was started with, "You are not broken, so we are not here to fix you." The facilitator went on to say, "You are going to have good thoughts and you are going to have bad thoughts. You may choose not to act on the bad thoughts and avoid bad situations that cause you and others problems or harm." The meeting was conducted by Gina Wolfe with the Cypress Initiative and she was my instructor through two graduations, along with a couple of other volunteers. She became, and is, a good friend. We continue to keep in touch, as I do with a few other guest instructors and speakers to the class. She still reminds me of lessons we learned in class to this day. It also taught me that you are going to have negative or bad thoughts, and you may choose to use your inner wisdom and not act on them or let them affect your state of mind. I also learned you have a higher success rate of applying for a job, asking for a raise, or selling something when your thoughts are good and your state of mind is at a higher level. The same could be said of not doing the above when you are in a low state of mind or having bad thoughts, a bad day if you will, as many people that were in a bad way had simply had a bad thought and used bad judgment and were now here at work release. I also came to know, or to see, that you are born with a free will and wisdom that you have had since birth, which is always with you if you choose to hear it and or use that inner wisdom. Second Chance also teaches that if you make decisions and interact with people when you're in a low state of mind, the outcome may not be as good if you were to make decisions and interact with people when you're in a good or a high state of mind. A couple of examples that relates to my own personal experiences is that the best time to sell something is right after you have sold something. You feel good about yourself; your confidence is high, and you are in a high state of mind. The same could be said for applying for a better job or asking for a raise or a promotion. You are much more apt to be successful in one of the above if you are in a positive state of mind and feel good about yourself: i.e. the best time to get a better job is when you have a good job you are happy with, or not asking for a raise when the bill collectors are calling and you and your spouse or significant other are quarreling. I think you get the gist of this. We were born with a God given talent, wisdom, and free will that cannot be taken away. If you are not happy doing what you're doing, then you are either not doing what you were born to do, or you need to adjust your thinking or perspective on things; sort of cleanse your thinking, so to speak, and get a new look at things. I know this because I have been about as low in my thinking as one can be, and I have been at the top of the world in my thinking, ready to accomplish anything. So can you!!! I will talk a little more about this in the final chapter.

My first job at work release was working at a towing company in Winter Haven, Florida, not too far from the work camp. I was working for an old friend, Billy Martino, who had owned a race track in Lakeland that my dealerships had a long business relationship with. Billy and I had never been that close during those times, but he was grateful for what I had done for the race track and gave me the job. I so enjoyed working with him, and we have become closer and still get together to solve all the problems of the world. While there, I did paperwork, dispatched wreckers, and answered the phone. It was a fairly secluded location and was perfect for my reentry to the working world. I knew several of the wrecker drivers coming in. Many knew they knew me but could not place me in that environment, so they would ask if they knew me and I would just tell them I don't think so. This was the perfect reentry job with just enough of the car business to keep things interesting.

I had been working there about two months or so when the "press" struck again. I received a phone call from the local reporter who had been covering my story. The reporter asked if Michael Holley worked there. I said yes but he was not here, as I was instructed by DoC not to talk to the press without the permission of DoC. I was actually answering the phone and signing paperwork as Randall Holley, using my middle name to stay below the radar. She then called the work camp and told them I was not at work and wanted to know if I was at the work camp, which is the same as reporting that I had "escaped." So they came and pick me up and took me back to the work camp. Someone from Demilly came over in a van, shackles in hand, with my "face sheet" and was about to shackle me and take me back to prison. The major that was over this work release camp called me in and ask my side of the story. I told her I had never broke a DoC rule and was not going to when I was that close to the end of my ordeal. I also told her that I had never stepped out of the gate of the compound where I worked, and if anyone wanted to check, the lot was under 24/7 security camera surveillance. They never did, but the Major and whomever she was talking to on the phone seemed satisfied that I did not break any rules and could stay at the work release center but could not return to my job, as DoC was not happy with the press coverage. The reporter published my pay and questioned my relationship with car people that might be associated with the wrecker company. None of it was true, of course, but I did not expect that to change.

So, I guess after being faced with being back in a prison "behind the wire," I was so relieved that it did not happen that I almost overlooked the fact that it had cost me my job. Yes, I lost that job over a reporter's phone call; giving a whole new meaning to "the power of the press." After that, every job I came up with was either turned down or not acted on. I would be sequestered to the work release compound for about a month. So I spent the next month not working but taking care of the lawn at the camp, and I enjoyed mowing the lawn. In passing, the major said the lawn looked great, and I said that is because it was mowed with love; and I meant it. I truly did love the fact that I was still at work release and mowing the lawn with some degree of freedom.

One day as I was mowing the lawn, I was in a very good state of mind, and it came to me that the best thing I could do for work was what I had learned to do at the Cabinet Shop at Hamilton CI. It would be something DoC should be happy with, and it would give me a chance to work with what I had learned. So I called a friend in construction, John, owner of a local construction company. I asked if he knew of a cabinet shop where I could work. He made some calls, and I was hired at A Ward Design, an all wood custom cabinet and casework shop in Winter Haven, Florida, owned by Kevin Ward. The major and DoC were happy with this and signed off on it in days. The shop was well off the beaten path and not easily accessible. Although, in time, the press would harass him about my working there. To this day, it still amazes me how the press is so relentless for a story; regard for people's lives becomes irrelevant if it suits their purpose and sells some papers.

Just after the 4th of July, I was building and helping assemble very high-end cabinets. The DoC was happy with the selection, and I worked there for the next five months until I completed work release; working up to my last day in work release. I had never really worked with my hands, and I was very fortunate to work with some very talented craftsmen on the design, building, and finishing of these cabinets. My wife says, that I cannot change a light bulb. So I was pretty proud of the fact that I was working in a high-line cabinet shop. I do not pretend to be a master craftsman, because I am not, but there is something rewarding about working with your hands, the work and quality of what came out of that shop

I would put up against any in the world. It is a world apart from the business world that I came from, but it is very rewarding to see the projects come together and move out the door. I never saw a finished project, in person, as it was against the rules to leave the cabinet shop to go to installs, but they brought me back pictures. We did good work, and they still do.

At this camp, although minimum security, I would witness three more shakedowns in the time I was there. The first was within weeks of my arrival, but was pretty mild. There wasn't as much, or almost no yelling and screaming. We were just taken to the chow hall and searched while they checked the dorm. During the second shakedown, I was in the "working dorm," meaning everyone that had a job and was contributing half their pay to DoC. I'm not complaining, mind you, I was happy to give half my pay and be at this camp. This dorm was air conditioned, as were all the dorms in work release. This shakedown was a little more intense. We were strip searched and then taken to the chow hall to await the outcome of the search. I think they searched every dorm and the compound with dogs. The next day, I heard that they found a cell phone and some K2, fake marijuana, on the compound, but no one went back to prison, "jail," as the inmate count was the same the next day. They had the compound count, men staying on compound, on the office wall where we checked out, and I checked it every morning and evening; you know, trying to keep the brain active. I also helped the sergeant do inventory, cleaned up some files and storage rooms—anything to feel normal.

I graduated Second Chance class, but the program lost its funding. Our facilitator, along with a few others, continued to teach the next class at their own expense, and I acted as a graduate assistant by helping those who wanted to complete the course and graduate. My interaction with these young, and sometime older, men and the heartfelt appreciation they had for the class was one of the most rewarding experiences in my life. There is no greater reward than to give of yourself, to help others. I gave very little and received much. There was one particular student that approached me several times; he just did not get what was being said. He was reading one of the books from the Second Chance class, written by Sydney Banks, and he said, "I just don't get it." I said, "You're focusing too hard on the words. Just read and let your mind go. It's not about the words, it's about the feelings and thoughts. It's about seeing what you can't presently see and hearing what you can't presently hear." Within the next couple of weeks he came running up to me very excited and said, "I get it! I get it!" Then at graduation, this very shy, very socially immature young man stood up and gave one of the most eloquent from the heart talks about his experiences in class, what it meant to him, and how he would get through life without any more trouble.

The readmission rate to the Florida Department of Corrections is all over the board. I read a number of reports in preparation for this book, both state and national. Put it all together and it is over fifty percent, in some categories as high as seventy five percent with hundreds of variables. It is a fact, regardless of the study you read, that the readmission rate of those that complete programs like vocational education, adult education classes, Second Chance or other faith-based reentry program's run by outside volunteers, could be about half of those who do not. So many of the inmates I encountered while in the Department of Corrections, regardless of the facility, are simply people that had very little structure, education, or positive interaction with people who truly wanted to help them. Many simply need a plan and a way to see that there is a possibility that they can succeed. I currently interact with prison support groups and those who teach faith-based reentry programs, and there is no doubt of the impression made by volunteers or someone who cares enough to contribute their time and show that they're willing to help. There is oodles of proof that it does work. Faith based learning, facilitated by someone who truly wants them to do better and succeed, goes a very long way with those about to reenter society, and it should be offered to every inmate that will leave a corrections facility. For the record, every inmate does go through a reentry program/class, but in many cases, those taught by DoC guards just do not have the same effect; so you have the readmissions rate that you have. DoC is well aware of the success rate of certain outside groups that teach reentry, and it is moving at getting everyone that will reenter society through one of these classes with a proven success record. In the end, it is cheaper than the price of sending them back to prison. But again, you are dealing with a very big bureaucracy that moves very slowly; and you have to wonder if it is every person's goal in DoC to have a low reentry rate. It is often discussed that the prison system is big business for someone, and although the prisons act as if they are on a shoestring budget, the prison system is a big budget item, over two billion dollars in fiscal year 2013 in Florida. With 1.7% dedicated to education and programs, everyone eligible should get to go to work release for their last six months. You give half your pay to DoC for participating in work release, so if run correctly, it should be a money maker for the prison system. Plus, it helps the inmate to get in the proper state of mind to be released. It is also a better environment to teach reentry, drug programs, or anger management than from behind the wire.

The remainder of my time in work release I worked, read books, was able to have eight hour furloughs at home on Saturdays, and go to my own church on Sundays for a few hours. Visitation at the camp was laid back and more enjoyable than "behind the wire." The sergeants, officers, and staff at the work release all treated me with respect and kindness. Most seemed to really care about the outcome of the inmates. We had a few problem inmates there, but they would usually trip up and get sent back to prison.

I believe in God, and believe there is always a bigger plan. I will tell you that Second Chance class changed me forever, or completed an ongoing process. I was allowed to see more and understand things that were so foreign to me in the past. I was able to use and expand my ability to interact with people of all walks of life, to see and understand so many of the hearts and souls of the young men that I had been surrounded with for the last twenty months. It was not so much like a bolt of lightning that I received from the class or this group of people, but a culmination of the events, conversations, and people I had been interacting with since my ordeal started in October of 2008. This class just brought all those thoughts and feelings together so that I could more clearly see where I had been and where I was going. If it is to be my destiny, I truly do want to help those that seek to know more, see more, and be more in this short life here on earth.

"Time is money."

— Benjamin Franklin

17

A SEMI-FREE BUT ENLIGHTENED NEW MAN

On December 16, 2011, at 12:37 a.m. I walked out of the Bartow Work Release Center a free man, or at least that's what I thought. December 14th was my wife's birthday that I missed again for the second year. This last couple of months had been particularly grueling for her, as she was finishing up the first of two Master's degrees that she had been working on. She was also responsible for getting me to and from work on most days, because she and my boss, Kevin Ward, were the only two approved to drive me to work; DoC did not provide transportation. I cannot believe the sacrifices she has made during the last three years since the collapse of our world began, and the attitude, leadership, and love she has shown through it all.

I worked my last day at the cabinet shop on Thursday, December the 15th. The Wards had a barbeque lunch for me, and it was hard to believe that I had only worked there for just under six months. I had learned and experienced so much. Everyone I worked with was very special, many taking the time to teach me much about their trade. For this time, and the people at Ward's that made it possible, I am very grateful. Once again, I was provided with numerous guardian angels that helped me through yet another step on my new journey.

Final graduation of the Second Chance program at Bartow work release was also Thursday night December 15th, as there was no more funding, and to this date it is not being taught at work release centers in Polk, that I am aware of. Gina Wolf had a graduation program for the second or third time since I had arrived, and all the inmates were very grateful for her efforts. She remains a close and trusted friend, as it is also her destiny to help others see what they do not see and hear what they do not hear, all while making better decisions in life. I would like to see schools, corporations, and church groups that like to give, take up a Second Chance type class, because people deserve a Second Chance. I understand that, as of this writing, there is an expansion of the faith based reentry programs in Florida. They are based on proven results by proven groups and facilitators. I hope and pray to soon be one of the facilitators of one of these types of programs. Just weeks ago, I met with the Chaplain at Polk CI to discuss just that. I also hope and pray that this book serves as a platform for me and others to expand the scope for all of those in need.

Words cannot express what it was like to be going home. My wife, Hope, and my son, Christopher, picked me up at the facility, and we drove home. Wow, what a feeling to sleep in my own bed. I had not slept in my own bed for 615 nights. But who's counting? Me, that's who!

For the last nine months, I was truly in a "reentry" mode or program, having gone home on Saturdays and allowed to attend my own church on Sundays. Any piece of anything that could make you feel normal was gratifying, but to walk out of this facility a free man was a feeling beyond belief. A Cuban friend once told me, "It is one thing to be free, it is yet another to have never been free, but to know freedom and lose that freedom is an experience few will ever have." Thank God! He lived in Cuba before communism and after communism. Then he migrated to the United States. He knew first hand of this experience. Now he says he has an appreciation of freedom in the US. So having experienced what I experienced, I could not even comprehend those in free countries taken over and the loss of that freedom, such as the Jewish, Polish or French people in WWII, or a POW. None of them had a release date, or even worse, would never be released. So as bad as this was, you do have to bring it into perspective with other events that have happened.

Remember earlier in the book I mentioned I had a bunch of probation that would be waived or terminated when all the conditions of the plea-bargain agreement were met? All the conditions were met, meaning full restitution paid, court order to protect credit in place. However, I would not be released from probation without another series of battles and hearings. It seems like it took forever, but in fact it took a little over three months. But that's another story.

I cannot express the emotions that I had as we drove home. The only thing that I could say was that it was so good to be home sleeping in my own bed after a little over twenty months or 615 days, 14 hours and 40 minutes since leaving that courtroom. After waking up on Friday, it was a busy day. I had my hearing to release probation (didn't happen), and all convicted felons had to report to the Sheriff's Department within twenty-four hours in Florida. We also had a family dinner planned for that night. Needless to say today, I am free. For a guy that had never been in trouble with the law to go through this experience was truly like a nightmare. Or to use the analogy that I used earlier in the book, the best fiction writer on their best day could not have written this story. I was so glad to be home with my family and to start trying to figure out how to start over. As it turned out, at least for the short while, I would go back to work for my friend's towing company and help him open up a used car lot, until such time as I can sort out my life. But for now, I was home with my family and friends, and that alone was the most important thing. I can now go to church without being on a time limit. I can go to the grocery store. I still love to walk through Publix's to see who I see. I was so excited to not be in a hurry, or just drive a car down the street. Within a few days of coming home, I was faced with more tragic news. My uncle, Capt. Richard Holley, my dad's younger brother, my mentor who I had apprenticed under for my captain's license, was terminally ill and was not expected to live much longer. During my court hearing on the day of my release, the judge approved my travel outside of the county (remember I'm on probation), which meant I could go see my uncle before he passed.

As I left my house in the wee hours of the morning to go pick up my sister and drive to Panama City, Florida for one last visit with my uncle, I passed the hospital on the way out of town and realized I forgot to get gas. I pulled in to get gas. A policeman had been shot a day or so earlier and had passed away. Leaving the hospital was a huge police escort that was moving the body and the family to another location. I do not know how many police officers were in cars or on motorcycles, but it was a lot of them. As the procession passed by, I sat at the gas station and began to cry uncontrollably about everything. More than anything in the world I wanted to be home, to be there when my family awoke. I knew even though my uncle's hours were limited on this earth he, being one of the greatest fathers I have ever witnessed, would understand that in my short freedom I felt the need to be with my family. He died the next day, and I would drive to Panama City to attend his funeral the day after Christmas on my fifty-first birthday. He was a man of great faith, a man of the sea, a great and loved captain, an author, and a husband. But his greatest God given talent was as a father and grandfather. He was promoted to glory where he and my father are awaiting all of us in the heavens until that time when we should all be reunited.

"It takes many good deeds to build a good reputation, and only one bad one to lose it."

— Benjamin Franklin

18

BACK TO BUSINESS AND
SEEKING TO HELP OTHERS

I n the first three or four months of being released, I spent a large amount of time and financial resources obtaining the probation, which I believed to be automatic, release. Except for a few loose ends and a few court costs, everything had been paid before I took the plea agreement on April 9th, and the Federal Court order to restore credit history had been completed without one single documented complaint. At the first hearing on the day of my release, the attorney for the government argued that I cannot get off probation because I was not on probation. He said that I had to report in to the process before it could be terminated. After the judge quoted some case law, she concurred and told me to report to my probation officer, and they would schedule a new hearing in the future for the release. The problem is when you're on probation, the probation department, still part of DOC, is not going to endorse or recommend early termination of probation without having your case evaluated and confirming for themselves all items of probation has been completed, which is not unreasonable on their part. Remember what I said: in DOC things do not move fast. My probation officer was more than understanding and helped me through the process of understanding early termination from the department's view. He stated the plea agreement stated that probation "may" be terminated early. He then explained that it needed to say probation "shall" be terminated early. So I guess it was a "what comes first the chicken or the egg." This was another test of my patience, and yet another humbling experience. After accumulating quite a few additional legal bills that I did not have the money to pay for, probation was ultimately released on March 26, 2012, after much bantering between my legal team and the same young prosecutorial attorney as the December 16th hearing. I was now off to start my new life. I only point out the above to show that nothing involving a government agency happens quickly or with any common sense. It is not a personal thing against the people inside the agency that is involved; small things or even big things just seem to take on a life of their own. I hold no personal animosity towards those involved, and most seemed very nice and just wanted to do the right thing within the agency in which they worked, subject to a little personal sabre rattling.

I must point out that the same reporter who had followed my case with a vengeance was waiting for me and my wife as we exited the courtroom. She seemed crushed when I, not so nicely, declined an interview and my attorneys escorted me into the waiting elevator. I do understand that everyone who I thought had their own agenda or angle in my case would also have their own version of events. As I stated earlier in the book, if I had been forthcoming with all my problems and given the painful interviews that the media wanted me to, this might have had a different outcome. For that, the blame lies solely with me, and I accept that responsibility without excuses. I have and do ask for forgiveness for it, keeping in mind this journey had not been without its own rewards, education, and enlightenment. I truly did have a new perspective on life and my future journey.

One caveat to all of this is that even though I made many bad decisions, and my judgment on much was incorrect, I did not take any money. Not only did I not personally benefit from my bad decisions, but I lost everything I had worked so hard for. One forensic auditor for GMAC during the days of October 2008 stated to someone in the office that everything was so organized and easy to find that nothing was hid, and although the company was insolvent there was nothing missing or out of place; we concealed nothing. We were just broke as would be many others in the coming year. When I received the box of discovery that had been turned over to my attorneys, there were no bank records that had been subpoenaed and gone though. So I suspect that most knew I might have mismanaged but not personally taken any money or benefited from the business failure. During all this I received a hand written envelope from the IRS doing an audit. My tax return for 2007 was about an inch and a half thick and they found no irregularities. I only owed a little money for a miscalculated interest deduction. But that was just more water under bridge. It is now just a history book to be read and learned from but never changed.

I worked at the used car lot and wrecker service in Winter Haven, where I had worked for a short time in work release, until an opportunity came to open a business with a longtime friend. My friend, Steve Schmidt, and I opened a used car lot in Lakeland Florida, just a half mile from where my world had collapsed in October of 2008. I have to say, as much as I dreamed about being back in the car business, I was never happy with the day-to-day operations of a small used car lot. I was so worried about Steve's investment in this new business. It had nothing to do with his actions or adapting, it was just my own inner worries and concerns, the constant worries of the past or even the future. We had a great business concept, The New Car Alternative, I still believe in the concept.

My friend, Derrick Kelley, told me returning to the retail car business in the same town where all the past had transpired was therapy for getting exposed to and reengaged with the public. There was some press coverage about my reentry into the car business, and Steve's going from newspaper business to the car business, but for the most part it was fairly mundane and even positive compared to the mutilations of the past—except for a TV reporter who put someone on the air holding papers in there hand saying they were wronged, and that I should never again be allowed in the car business. I still have all my notes from all the complaints and proceeding, and this person's name never appeared, not in criminal, civil, or bankruptcy court. So the TV station just gave someone an audience just because they could, and again the facts were, well you know... "Never let the facts get in the way of a good story."

The one thing about being in the public eye and in retail is that it does give those a chance, I mean anyone, to stop in and speak their mind. I had so many uplifting, positive, and yes almost spiritual encounters with so many strangers and past acquaintances that words do not do it justice. Businessmen that had been in trouble or lost businesses, some hardcore, maybe even not nice people by their own admission, had found the Lord and found a different course for their lives. Broke and tired, many decided that their journey was in a different direction. Some said they were just touched by a feeling or a thought to stop by and say hello and see how I was doing. For a stranger to come in and just want to say hello to see how I was doing and tell me that they are glad I was okay was such a blessing. Many said they had and were praying for me and my family; this makes an impression that ink on paper cannot express. For someone to tell you that the Lord touched their heart for them to just stop by and have a conversation is a blessing that I did not take lightly. Their actions, for whatever reason, created emotions beyond my ability to express myself or show the appreciation I felt. So many were so supportive with so many prayers and best wishes.

This ordeal, financial collapse, loss of my businesses, and loss of my freedom had now consumed five years of my life. I like to put it this way: what took me and my employees, management team, and financial institutions twenty five years to build was dismantled in three months. I spent hundred hour weeks, seven day work weeks including nights, getting by on just a few hours' sleep so I could be at the office by 4 a.m. to make a deal that was not possible ultimately become a reality. This is a world, the burning desire to succeed, that few are exposed to or understand. I now hope to help some of them achieve their dreams.

Entrepreneurs are often a strange breed with a drive to succeed that is just very difficult to comprehend. So many have the desire, the idea, but lack the drive to get it done at all cost. Somewhere there is a room full of what almost was, but the person, the inventor, the entrepreneur quit the day before the success. This country would not be what it is without the drive and risk taking that seems to be a common if not required trait of an "entrepreneur."

Yes, the next bestselling book, the award winning movie script, the cure for some awful disease, even the next great app or public company is in someone's desk, banker's trash can, hard drive or on the invention table waiting to be fulfilled. You and your idea are a success waiting to happen until you let someone talk you out of what is due you if you have the perseverance to succeed.

One of the great compliments that I received during these impromptu visits from past customers was people telling me about the charity or sponsorships provided to them, or a friend, or an organization, or church they were affiliated with. The events, trips, or programs that had occurred, or might not have been, if not for our funding or providing something. I knew that I was rarely the one to do these things, but someone in my organization had, and that meant more to me than having donated it myself. Giving and caring can become a culture just like not doing so. I was very happy to hear these stories of those that had been helped and those in my organization that did the right thing for such deserving and appreciative people. I truly wish, in spite of going broke, we had given and done more. I once heard a very wealthy man say, "Those that die with the most toys win." That is so sad and so untrue. There are no U-Haul trailers full of toys attached to the hearse. The true joy in success is the ability to do more and give more to those that are in need. For those that do like to help or give, remember we do not pick those in need, so give when your heart says give, not when the brain thinks it politically correct or intellectually prudent.

After again experiencing automotive retail, after we sold out, my friend and partner deciding to return to the newspaper business. I decided it was time to soul search and decide what I wanted to be and where I wanted to end up "when I grow up." And yes, at fifty-plus years old we are still learning, maturing, and even worse, still making mistakes and figuring out God's chosen path for us in life. That is very difficult when you've only chosen two career paths in life, one as a boat captain and the other a car dealer. Now with my new found wisdom and enlightenment, I have to look deep inside and decide there must be something else. So it was at Monsignor John Caulfield's funeral on November 7, 2013, sitting with my wife and between two longtime friends, Cody Lowry and Jimmy Dean, I decided to make this major change in life.

The beginning of this change is before you now. I have been approached by a number of people who have family members who are incarcerated seeking counsel, others of whom were graduates of the Second Chance class, and wish to do more. Then there are the prison support groups, faith-based reentry programs, prison ministries, public speaking, and life coaching. Lastly, is my ability to consult, coach, and mentor business owners and entrepreneurs, both automotive and other businesses on how to expand and acquire, to reduce the size or restructure, or plan an exit strategy, by helping them do what they wish successfully and with a plan. I like giving owners, managers, CEO's, board members, and entrepreneurs a new and enlightened perspective. For a simple and uneducated man, I have experienced much in this life. I love sharing it with you and for you. God's gift of my ability to speak to hundreds without fear is a gift I have never taken lightly. I am working on my ability to be a self-published author and publisher and to learn the trade so that I might help others with their unrealized dream.

I truly believe that next year's best seller or solution to someone's problem is in a manuscript in a desk drawer or on a hard drive waiting to be realized or published, after rejection by others.

Something that I would like to see is for Second Chance Class or a faith based reentry class to be available for all inmates, and taught in a faith based environment by outside volunteers, churches, or organizations; maybe also in churches and communities for people that might need a second chance but are not yet in trouble with the law. I feel it is important to teach someone that they do not necessarily have to make that bad decision, act on that bad thought, or use that bad judgment and wind up where they don't want to be and where they are a burden as opposed to being a contributor. I want to teach them that being a father or mother and a productive member of our society is far more rewarding than trying to learn or figure out how to reenter society. So the decision I have made is to do all of the above where I am asked to do it or where I can find an audience or platform to use it; and to write this book from the heart, as a thank you to all of my guardian angels who have helped me get to this point in my life and helped me succeed at touching others in the remainder of my journey. I want to sit with that businessman who is looking at growth or an exit strategy and say, let's look at this from a different and fresh perspective. I also want to help businessmen and women who might be in trouble, or be on the verge of making mistakes that might, as I did, take on a life of their own.

My experiences were meant to be shared, and yes sometimes that is painful, sometimes it is rewarding, and sometimes people just need a different view, a different perspective, if you will, in order to make the correct decisions for their family, employees, and/or stockholders. If I am the one they choose to help them with business or personal decisions, speak to a group, or just help figure out how to make a work environment more enjoyable for everyone while helping the company be more profitable or stable, it would be a great way to work for the rest of my life. I love to work with and interact with people, I draw strength from those interactions. Whether it is one, ten thousand, or any number in-between it is an honor and a pleasure to share, teach, and explain how I accomplished what I did, how to avoid the pitfalls of rapid growth and unchecked mistakes, and that building relationships in life is priceless and pays many dividends. Learning what not to do is just as an important lesson as learning what to do. It is important to establish business and ethical principles that must be followed regardless of the drive to success or downturns in life. Honoring and loving your family and friends is the highest and most respected principle you can have.

One question I am asked frequently, using different words with the same meaning, has been, "How are you so normal after all you've been through?" First, normal is in the eyes of the beholder and wide open to interpretation, and there are a lot of complicated answers about this. The very simple truth is that it's an easy one though, and that is "faith, family and friends," and my love of people is so strong it could not be tarnished by any manmade circumstance. My faith and free will are so a part of my heart that no person of this earth can take it away. Of all the Bible verses that I have read, and there are many, one stands above the rest, and it has given me as much comfort as any other: 1 Corinthians 13:13, "And now these three remain: faith, hope and love. But the greatest of these is love."

I ask for forgiveness from all those, or their families, who I have harmed, and I forgive all of those who wished ill will on me or my family. I ask for forgiveness from the many employees and companies that were such a large part of the success of my companies, and even though I may have never properly expressed it, I clearly see that I and my company would not have become what it did without you.

In the end, I cannot help what others believe or what others think, and I certainly have no control over the thoughts others have. They cannot know what are in my thoughts, intentions, or my heart, just as I cannot know what are in theirs. I believe that in helping others we help ourselves. There is not a person that I encountered inside the Department of Corrections, officers, civilians or inmates, not one group I have interacted with or spoke to that I did not and do not get more out of the experience than I give. I am the one uplifted and driven to do more for those that seek more. When I speak to a group, it is I who feel lifted and motivated when I leave the room. The valuable lesson in this is that it is truly greater to give than receive, to help others than to receive help. Know this, you cannot give what you do not have. Remember on the airplane when they announce to put on your oxygen mask first then help others. So it is in life: to give money you must have it, to give wisdom you must access what you have inside you to share, to give love you must have and experience love, and lastly, to share your experiences you must first have those experiences. May you savor the good and learn the lesson from the bad, and share both with everyone that will listen. May God's blessings be on the rest of your journey that we call life.

³⁵ For I was hungry and you gave me food, I was thirsty and you gave me drink, I was a stranger and you welcomed me, ³⁶ I was naked and you clothed me, I was sick and you visited me, I was in prison and you came to me. ³⁷ Then the righteous will answer him, saying, 'Lord, when did we see you hungry and feed you, or thirsty and give you drink? ³⁸ And when did we see you a stranger and welcome you, or naked and clothe you? ³⁹ And when did we see you sick or in prison and visit you?' ⁴⁰ And the King will answer them, 'Truly, I say to you, as you did it to one of the least of these my brothers, you did it to me.'

Matthew 25: 35-40

ACKNOWLEDGEMENTS

I would like to give thanks to all those who had a hand in the creation of this book. First and foremost I give thanks to God for all the blessings I have been given and for all the guardian angels who have ushered and counseled me to this point in my life. As so many authors before me have said, and it is so accurate, that writing a book is hard work and takes the patience of a lot more people than just the writer. This book would not have been written without the support of my wife, Hope, and the constant encouragement of Christopher, Trey, and Carter. To my mom Joyce for the upbringing, love and constant support and more ways than there are words to write. To her husband Wayne, thank you for always being there. Thank you to my in laws, Richard and Dee, whose home I outlined, dictated, and laid out this book while in seclusion at their Georgia home on a cold winter weekend in January and the constant support and encouragement.

Thank you to all those who were part of my life from the time I was born to the conclusion of this book, constantly molding and steering me through this journey. The list is long but I must pay special tribute to the Davis family, the late Bill Hughes, my first football coach, the pastors and congregation of the Lynn Haven Presbyterian Church. To Pastor Jay Dennis of First Baptist Church at the Mall, whose letter of October 23, 2008 I still carry with me everywhere I go, the prayers and encouragement are still helping me. To all those I worked with on the boats growing up, to the employees of Tommy Thomas Chevrolet, and of course to L.E. "Tommy" Thomas and his family and extended family, I will always be grateful for all that was done for an ambitious and immature child who aspired to be more. My thanks, love and appreciation for the large list of employees, managers and customers of T. Thomas

Chevrolet, Michael Holley Chevrolet KIA Pontiac Buick GMC, many of which I now just call "friend".

The list is so long on all of those that contributed to my learning and success it would take another book to list. But to those that absolutely taught me, guided me, and supported me for the last twenty-five years of business, I say thank you.

To the guardian angels of the last five or so years, thank you and God bless you for getting me through and lifting me up. A special thank you to Linda Zimmerman, Frank Meredith, Eva Stewart, may she rest in peace, Steve and Cheryl Schmidt, Dennis Hood, my sister Sally Poteete, Billy Martino, Derrick Kelley, Pat Fischer, James and Linda Barber, Katie and Eric Decker, Doc and Paula Dockery, Kim and Seth McKeel. To Bill Parry, may he rest in peace, Gene Casey and Mary Ellen Self who each wrote me weekly for twenty months. To Randy Roberts and Gerry McHugh who were with me prior to their untimely deaths and still are, may you both rest in peace. Also to our large and extended "baseball family" headed by Coach Len Brutcher. Thank you to the St. Joseph Catholic Church family and its current Pastor Ramon Bolatete who seem to always have a kind welcoming word and open arms and so many more.

Now to those with whom this project you see before you would not have been possible. My many thanks to my first two editors, my wife Hope and her mom Dee; to those that read and served as my peer group reviewers: Joe Flumerfelt, Dave Hansen, Dan Oxford, Jim Quinlan, Edward Peterson, Roch D'Aoust and Gina Wolf; to my web designer, constant motivator, and un-paid publicist, Maulissa Rampersad of RubbernGlue.com; to my friend Jim Quinlan for writing the Foreword from his heart to these pages; to my editor Elizabeth Pace of Pace Editing; to the cover designer, Laura Cooper of Art Works; to the photographer Jason Katz owner of J&J Photography; and to all who did what they did for free or reduced charges so that this book could be.

Lastly, for my many coaches that helped in getting this book started and helping me stick with it to its completion, I could not have done this without your lessons, coaching and encouragement.

Dan Poynter of Para Publishing is truly the Godfather of self-publishing. Dan, I read all your books and newsletters, some twice. Thank you for the encouraging emails! Tony Gaskins, your online course helped me get motivated to lay it all out and get started, your conversations and emails encouraged me, thank you. Lastly to my constant motivator and chief guardian angel, Monsignor John Caulfield, may he rest in peace. Finally, to all who had advice, input, prayers or encouragement, and those that pre-ordered thank you, and may God Bless you.

To contact Michael Holley with comments, questions or just to send a word of encouragement you may email him at Michael@ michaelholley.com

To inquire about speaking engagements, consulting, business/ life coaching, private book signings or attendance at your corporate or private event you may email him direct, call Hopeful Publishing at (844) 446-7338 or send an inquiry form at www. hopefulpublishing.com.

Sign up for Michael's newsletters at www.michaelholley.com
Follow Michael's blog at www.michaelholley.com/blog
Friend him on Facebook, LinkedIn, Twitter and Goodreads

Michael R. Holley
"The Engager"
Business Consultant, Speaker, Author, Life/Business Coach
email:Michael@michaelholley.com

Pricing for Speaking, Consulting and Business/Life Coaching on request.

Upcoming books from Hopeful Publishing Company, Inc.
By Michael R. Holley

"The Engager's Perspective on the Art of Building Business Relationships" 2015
"The Engager's Perspective on the Dying Art of Compromise" late 2015
"The Engager on the Dying Art of Common Sense" 2016
"The Engager's Perspective on Political Correctness Out of Control" 2017

We are looking for the book or manuscript inside your desk drawer or on your hard drive that you thought would never be published.

Speaking to and inspiring those who desire to do more while helping others!

Made in the USA
Charleston, SC
27 January 2015